SELF-CARE RX FOR HEALTHCARE PROFESSIONALS

PROVEN STRATEGIES TO COMBAT STRESS AND BURNOUT

CHRIS WAGNER RN BSN

CONTENTS

Introduction	v
1. Proactivity And Resilience in Healthcare	1
2. Mastering Emotion Regulation in Healthcare	14
3. The Paradox of Comfort	26
4. Embracing Nature's Healing	36
5. Financial Well-being and Mental Health	45
6. Engaging in Authentic Human Connection	57
7. Weathering the Storm: Strategies for Dealing with Difficult Patients and Families	66
8. Navigating Complex Patient Relationships and Setting Boundaries	77
9. Navigating Grief and Loss	88
10. The Role Of Continuing Education And Growth	98
Conclusion	109
Acknowledgments	111
About the Author	113
Bibliography	115

Copyright/Disclaimer:

All rights to this literary work, Copyright © 2023, are reserved to Chris Wagner. It is expressly prohibited to reproduce any part of this book in any format, including electronic or mechanical, without prior written consent from the author, except for brief quotations used in a book review.

Please be advised that both the publisher and the author are providing this book and its contents "as is," with no express or implied representations or warranties of any kind, including but not limited to fitness for a particular purpose. Any such representations and warranties are hereby disclaimed. Furthermore, neither the publisher nor the author assumes any responsibility for any errors, inaccuracies, omissions, or inconsistencies contained in this work.

Any information provided in this book should be independently verified and validated before acting upon it.

While this publication is intended to be a valuable source of information for readers, it is not intended to replace the advice and guidance of expert professionals. Should you require a high level of assistance, it is recommended that you seek out a competent professional.

Finally, it should be noted that the publisher and author of this book do not guarantee any level of success or results from following the advice and strategies provided. Any results will vary according to each individual's unique situation.

Printed in America

Editor: Pagetrim Book Edit & Design

ISBN — Ebook: 979-8-218-31571-9

ISBN – Paperback: 979-8-86646-345-9

INTRODUCTION

The realm of healthcare, historically demanding and emotionally taxing on both its patients and providers, faced an unprecedented challenge with the onset of the COVID-19 pandemic. The relentless demands, coupled with the outbreak, pushed the resilience and mental fortitude of our healthcare professionals to its limits. As the world watched in admiration and gratitude, many healthcare heroes reached a breaking point, with burnout rates skyrocketing. Tragically, many chose to walk away from the profession they once loved, feeling overwhelmed and unsupported. Even now, as we navigate the aftermath and ongoing challenges, healthcare professionals continue to experience burnout at alarming rates.

As a psychiatric registered nurse, I find myself at the crossroads of this crisis daily. I've witnessed first hand colleagues from various disciplines, once vibrant and passionate, going through the motions, their enthusiasm dimmed, their smiles downturned. The sparkle in their eyes, symbolic of the excitement with which they entered the profession, seems clouded by fatigue and discouragement.

It's against this backdrop that this book comes into existence. The goal is straightforward yet deeply consequential: to offer healthcare profes-

INTRODUCTION

sionals a toolkit to combat the intense stress and burnout that's become common in their roles. Through a blend of personal experiences, actionable strategies, and insights into mental well-being, this book seeks to rekindle the faded passion and provide a beacon during challenging times.

A healthcare professional's journey is undoubtedly one of profound impact and deep commitment. Yet, it's also one where the caregiver must prioritize their own well-being to sustainably care for others. This book is a testament to that journey, aiming to nurture the mind and spirit of those who have tirelessly given everything to the healthcare industry. While recognizing that employers also bear significant responsibility for the well-being of their staff, this book is designed to empower healthcare professionals with strategies within their control. There are many fields and work opportunities within healthcare, and sometimes a change in employment is the best solution. Through this book's pages, may you find the strength, passion, and balance to continue making a difference, one patient at a time.

Disclaimer: Throughout this book, readers will encounter stories and anecdotes designed to illustrate specific points or concepts. While some accounts are based on experiences, others are fictional and created for illustrative purposes. Any resemblance to actual persons, living or dead, or actual events is purely coincidental. The intention is to provide deeper understanding and insight, not to depict actual individuals or events. It's important to note that while this book focuses on individual empowerment and strategies, the role of employers in creating a healthy work environment is also paramount.

CHAPTER ONE
PROACTIVITY AND RESILIENCE IN HEALTHCARE

THE CRISIS OF REACTIVITY

IMAGINE THIS: You're in the middle of a hectic shift, juggling multiple responsibilities—reviewing patient medications, updating patient charts, and coordinating with other healthcare professionals. Suddenly, a patient's condition deteriorates rapidly. Alarms blare, colleagues rush in, and you find yourself in a flurry of activity, reacting to the crisis at hand. While you manage to stabilize the situation, the emotional and mental toll is undeniable. You're left drained, questioning your ability to face another such crisis. Sound familiar?

This scenario highlights the challenges of managing the often reactive nature of healthcare work. While swiftly responding to emergencies is a critical and necessary aspect of the job, constantly being in a mode of putting out fires, without the balance of preventative measures, can be problematic. Such continual reactivity can contribute to a range of negative outcomes, including medical errors and compromised patient care, and may ultimately lead to the burnout that is all too common in our profession.

THE COST OF MISTAKES

Let's consider a real-life example. A nurse, overwhelmed by the demands of her shift, administers the wrong dosage of medication to a patient. Thankfully, the error is caught in time, but the incident leaves both the nurse and the patient shaken. The nurse had been reacting to a backlog of tasks, rather than proactively managing her responsibilities. The result? A near-miss that could have had severe consequences.

Reactivity also serves as a stress multiplier. Each crisis you react to drains your emotional reserves, leaving you less equipped to handle the next challenge. It's a vicious cycle that feeds on itself, escalating stress levels and diminishing your ability to provide optimal care.

A study published in the Journal of Psychiatric Nursing, titled "Emotional Reactivity and Burnout in Clinical Nurses," identified a link between emotional reactivity and burnout levels in nurses. The research, led by Nihan Altan Sarıkaya et al., demonstrated that nurses with higher emotional reactivity are more susceptible to experiencing burnout. This finding highlights the critical need for addressing emotional reactivity to reduce burnout risks.

So, what's the alternative? How can we break free from this cycle of reactivity that seems almost ingrained in the healthcare culture? The answer lies in embracing proactivity and resilience, covered in this book and the focus of the chapters that follow.

By understanding the dangers of a reactive approach and learning to cultivate proactivity and resilience, you can not only safeguard your well-being but also elevate your practice, ensuring that you're not just surviving in your role but truly thriving.

THE PROACTIVE MINDSET

If reactivity is the quicksand that pulls us down, proactivity is the solid ground that allows us to stand tall. But what does it mean to be proactive in healthcare? At its core, proactivity is about taking control of your circumstances rather than being controlled by them. It's about anticipating challenges and preparing for them, rather than merely reacting when they occur.

THE PROACTIVE PRINCIPLE: A LESSON FROM STEPHEN COVEY

Stephen Covey, in his seminal book *The 7 Habits of Highly Effective People*, introduced the concept of the Proactive Principle.[2] Covey argues that our behavior is a function of our decisions, not our conditions. We have the ability to subordinate feelings to values, essentially choosing our response to any given situation. This principle is not just a business or self-help axiom; it's profoundly relevant in healthcare settings.

Imagine you're faced with a particularly challenging patient who is non-compliant with treatment plans. A reactive approach would be to get frustrated, perhaps even disengaged, thinking, "Why bother if they won't cooperate?" A proactive approach, guided by Covey's principle, would involve taking a step back and choosing your response. You might seek to understand the patient's reservations and work collaboratively to find a solution, not only improving patient care but also reducing your own stress levels.

Being proactive doesn't just make your workday smoother; it has tangible psychological benefits. Proactivity fosters a sense of autonomy, giving you control over your actions and, by extension, your stress levels. This sense of control is often cited as a key factor in avoiding burnout. When you're proactive, you're essentially writing your own script, choosing the narrative of your workday rather than having it dictated by external events.

Moreover, proactivity has a ripple effect. When you're proactive, you set a positive example for your colleagues, potentially shifting the entire team's mindset. This collective shift can lead to a more harmonious work environment, further reducing stress and enhancing job satisfaction.

In a profession where the stakes are high and the challenges many, adopting a proactive mindset can be your secret weapon. It empowers you to face difficulties head-on, armed with preparation and a positive outlook. As we navigate the subsequent chapters, we'll delve deeper into actionable strategies to cultivate this key trait, setting you on the right path to succeed in your healthcare career.

One of the cornerstones of a proactive mindset is the ability to anticipate. In healthcare, this skill is invaluable. Whether it's foreseeing potential complications in a patient's condition or predicting how changes in healthcare policy might affect your work environment, anticipation allows you to prepare and adapt. This readiness not only enhances patient care but also mitigates the stress associated with unexpected challenges and, ultimately, improves efficiency.

Being proactive also has a direct impact on emotional resilience. When you anticipate and prepare for challenges, you're less likely to be thrown off balance when difficulties arise. This emotional steadiness is crucial in a field where you're constantly exposed to human suffering and high-stakes decisions. It's not just about avoiding negative outcomes; it's about creating a mental space where you can operate at your best, even under pressure.

What's fascinating about proactivity is that it creates a positive feedback loop. Each successful anticipation of a challenge reinforces your belief in your ability to manage future challenges. This boosts your self-efficacy, further enhancing your proactive behavior. It's a virtuous cycle that not only improves your professional life but also enriches your personal well-being.

Let's not underestimate the impact of a proactive mindset on team dynamics. When one member of a healthcare team adopts a proactive approach, it often inspires others to do the same.

The collective benefit is exponential. Teams that operate proactively are more cohesive, more efficient, and less prone to conflict, creating an environment where both patients and healthcare providers flourish.

Proactivity is not just a quick fix; it's a long-term strategy that involves building a sustainable career in healthcare where you're not perpetually on the cusp of burnout. By adopting a proactive mindset, you're investing in your future, ensuring that you can sustainably provide exceptional care for years to come.

As we journey through this book, we'll explore various strategies to cultivate a proactive mindset, from mindfulness techniques to effective communication skills. We'll also explore actionable strategies to build resilience, from mindfulness exercises to peer support networks. If you've ever felt worn down by the relentless demands of your profession, the insights and strategies that follow could prove the catalyst for a more sustainable, fulfilling career in healthcare. But for now, let this serve as your introduction to the transformative power of proactivity in healthcare. If you've ever felt like you're constantly playing catch-up, always one step behind, then the insights and strategies that follow may prove the game-changers you've been seeking.

THE SYMBIOTIC POWER OF RESILIENCE AND PROACTIVITY

As we pivot from the proactive mindset, it's crucial to understand that proactivity and resilience are two sides of the same coin. They come as a package, like milk with your cornflakes. While proactivity equips you with the foresight to anticipate and prepare for challenges, resilience provides the grit and fortitude to bounce back when adversity strikes. In healthcare, where the emotional and physical toll can be immense, resilience isn't just a desirable trait; it's a lifeline.

But what does resilience look like in the context of healthcare?

It's the ability to maintain your emotional equilibrium when faced with a patient crisis. It's the inner strength that allows you to return to work, day after day, even when yesterday was a maelstrom of challenges.

Most importantly, it's the mental resilience that enables you to separate your sense of self-worth from the inevitable setbacks and failures that every healthcare professional encounters.

The beauty of resilience is that it amplifies the benefits of a proactive mindset. When you're proactive, you're less likely to encounter situations that test your resilience. And when those tests do come—as they inevitably will—your proactive preparations soften the impact and make it easier to bounce back. It's a symbiotic relationship where each quality enhances the other.

Consider a scenario where a proactive approach failed to prevent a crisis—a patient's sudden deterioration, for example. Resilience is what allows you to regroup, reassess, and re-engage with the situation, armed with the lessons learned from the experience. It's what enables you to face the next shift with renewed focus rather than dread. Moreover, resilience has a ripple effect similar to proactivity. A resilient healthcare professional serves as a role model, inspiring colleagues to adopt a similar mindset. This collective resilience can transform the entire work environment, making it more stable, supportive, collaborative, and ultimately, effective.

YOUR IMMEDIATE TOOLKIT: QUICK ACTIONS FOR COMBATING BURNOUT

Having explored the transformative power of proactivity and resilience, you might be wondering, "What can I do right now to combat this moment of burnout?" Here are some immediate, simple steps that encapsulate the essence of being both proactive and resilient.

THE MINDFUL MINUTE

Feeling overwhelmed? Take a 60-second pause. Close your eyes and focus on your breath. This isn't just a break; it's a moment of mindfulness that allows you to detach from the chaos, settle your nerves, and choose your next move deliberately. It's proactivity and resilience, condensed into one powerful minute of calm.

THE SINGLE STEP FORWARD

Ask yourself, "What's one thing I can control right now?" Then do it. Whether it's delegating a task or taking a sip of water, this immediate action is a proactive measure that gives you a small but significant sense of control, reinforcing your resilience in the process.

QUICK CONNECT

Send a brief message to a trusted colleague or friend, sharing your current emotional state. This act of reaching out is a resilient step, offering you a momentary emotional buffer. It also opens the door for support or advice, a proactive way to address what's causing your stress.

INSTANT GRATITUDE

In the midst of burnout, it's easy to lose sight of the positives.

Take 30 seconds to recall three aspects of your job that you're thankful for. This quick gratitude exercise can reframe your mindset, making you more resilient to current stressors and proactive toward seeking more of what fulfills you in your work.

These are your immediate tools, designed to be accessible the moment you feel the burden of burnout. They're small steps, but they're steeped in the principles of proactivity and resilience we've discussed.

Consider them your first line of defense, ready to deploy at a moment's notice.

THE BEDROCK OF RESILIENCE: PHYSICAL WELL-BEING

As we've delved into the concepts of proactivity and resilience, it's become evident that self-care is not just a supplement; it's foundational. And the foundation of any robust self-care regimen starts with your physical well-being.

In the demanding world of healthcare, it's easy to neglect our basic physical needs. We often find ourselves running on fumes, literally and metaphorically. But let's pause and consider the impact of this neglect. When you're physically drained, how well can you handle the emotional and mental challenges that come your way?

The answer is clear: not very well.

This is where the proactive approach comes into play. Instead of waiting for exhaustion to consume you, what if you took preventive measures? Adequate sleep, balanced nutrition, and regular exercise are not just checkboxes on a wellness list; they're proactive steps that prepare you for the inevitable challenges of your profession. By taking care of your physical health, you're not just preventing burnout; you're setting yourself up to be more resilient in the face of stressors that are part of healthcare.

In essence, your physical well-being is the bedrock upon which your resilience is built. It's the starting point that enables you to handle stress more effectively, make sound decisions, and provide the level of care your patients deserve. And as we'll see in the next sections, this physical foundation supports the emotional and social aspects of resilience, creating a holistic approach to self-care.

THE TRANSFORMATIVE POWER OF SLEEP

Matthew Walker's seminal work, *Why We Sleep*, sheds light on the profound, often underestimated impact of sleep on our overall well-being.[3] For healthcare professionals, who often find themselves in high-stakes, emotionally charged environments, the role of sleep becomes even more critical.

Walker's research reveals that sleep is not merely a passive state of rest; it's an active physiological process with a direct bearing on our cognitive and emotional faculties. Sleep enhances our ability to think clearly, make rational decisions, and manage stress—indispensable skills in the healthcare setting.

But the benefits of sleep go beyond cognitive enhancement.

Sleep serves as a natural form of emotional regulation. During the deep stages of sleep, our brain processes and neutralizes emotional experiences, effectively resetting our emotional compass for the next day. This "emotional first-aid" is particularly valuable for healthcare professionals, who often have to navigate their complex emotional landscapes and those of their patients.

In essence, sleep is a proactive form of self-care. By prioritizing quality sleep, you're not just preparing for the day ahead; you're equipping yourself with the emotional and cognitive tools needed to deal with the inherent stressors of healthcare. It's a form of resilience-building that starts in the bedroom and has knock-on effects throughout your professional and personal life.

BREAKING THE CYCLE: SLEEP, EMOTIONAL INTENSITY, AND STRESS

Building on the insights from Matthew Walker's *Why We Sleep*, it's crucial to understand the vicious cycle that can ensue between sleep deprivation, heightened emotional responses, and stress. When you're sleep-deprived, your brain's emotional centers become hyper-reactive, amplifying your emotional responses to challenging situations. This heightened emotional intensity can make the already stressful environment of healthcare even more overwhelming, leading to quicker burnout and diminished resilience.

But the cycle doesn't stop there. The increased stress from these emotionally charged situations can, in turn, lead to difficulties in falling asleep or staying asleep, perpetuating a destructive cycle of sleep deprivation and stress. This creates a downward spiral that not only affects your professional life but also seeps into your personal well-being, which can impact on your relationships with friends and family.

Breaking this cycle is imperative, and it starts with recognizing the red flags of burnout and taking proactive steps to address it. When you start to feel overwhelmed, it's crucial to pause and take a break. This isn't a sign of weakness; it's a proactive measure to protect your well-being and, by extension, the quality of care you provide. Whether it's stepping away for a few minutes to practice deep breathing or taking a day off to catch up on sleep, these breaks serve as circuit breakers in the stress-sleep deprivation cycle.

By prioritizing sleep and taking proactive breaks when needed, you're preventing burnout and, more importantly, actively building resilience.

You're equipping yourself with the emotional stability and cognitive clarity needed to navigate the complex, often stressful healthcare environment. Essentially, sleep becomes not just a form of rest but a critical tool in your resilience toolkit with far-reaching implications for your career and overall quality of life.

THE PROACTIVE APPROACH TO EXERCISE: OVERCOMING RESISTANCE

The transformative power of sleep, in building resilience cannot be understated, but another pillar that stands out as equally crucial is exercise. For healthcare professionals, who often find themselves physically and emotionally drained, the idea of engaging in strenuous physical activity may seem counterintuitive, if not downright unappealing. However, this is where the concept of proactivity comes into sharp focus.

James Clear's *Atomic Habits* offers a valuable lesson here: the first step is often the hardest, but also the most crucial.[4] According to Clear, the key to establishing any habit, including exercise, is to start small. The mere thought of going to the gym for someone who is tired and burned out can be off-putting. But what if you reframe it? Instead of focusing on the workout, focus on the first step: putting on your shoes and getting in the car. As Clear points out, once you've taken that initial step, the rest often falls into place. You're already out the door; you might as well go through with it.

This proactive approach to exercise is not just about physical fitness; it's a strategy for building resilience. Exercise releases endorphins, improves mood, and serves as a natural counterbalance to the stress and emotional toll of healthcare work. Or any work for that matter. By proactively incorporating exercise into your routine, you're not just improving your physical health but also fortifying your emotional and mental resilience.

The key takeaway here is that proactivity in exercise starts with overcoming the initial resistance. By focusing on that first, seemingly insignificant step, you set the stage for a cascade of positive actions that contribute to your resilience and overall well-being. And as we'll explore in subsequent sections, this proactive approach to physical well-being serves as a cornerstone for the emotional and social dimensions of resilience, offering a holistic approach to self-care.

REVERSING THE VICIOUS CYCLE: THE INTERCONNECTEDNESS OF STRESS, EXERCISE, AND SLEEP

Having looked at the complexities of resilience and its various dimensions and emphasizing the pivotal role that sleep and exercise play in nurturing and enhancing this fundamental aspect of human existence, it's important to understand how they are intricately connected in a cycle that can either be vicious or virtuous.

After a grueling day at work, the allure of escapism is strong. It's tempting to sink into the couch, binge-watch a series, and over-indulge in comfort food. While this might offer immediate gratification, it sets off a chain reaction that's detrimental in the long run. Lack of physical activity can contribute to insomnia, exacerbating your ability to cope with stress. You find yourself caught in a vicious cycle: stress leads to poor choices, leading to sleep deprivation, leading to heightened stress.

However, this cycle is not irreversible. By adopting proactive habits, you can turn it into a virtuous cycle. Imagine replacing that movie night with a brief exercise session. Exercise, as we've discussed, releases endorphins and serves as a natural stress-reliever. But the benefits don't stop there. Regular physical activity has been shown to improve sleep quality, making it easier for you to fall and stay asleep. Better sleep equips you with the emotional and cognitive tools to better handle stress, completing the circle in a positive loop.

The key to reversing this cycle lies in your proactive choices. Instead of succumbing to immediate gratifications that have long-term costs, opt for actions that offer long-term benefits. By making the conscious decision to replace unhealthy coping mechanisms with healthy ones, like exercise, it contributes to your resilience and overall well-being.

Fundamentally, by proactively incorporating healthy habits like exercise, you're not just breaking a vicious cycle; you're creating a virtuous one that enhances your resilience, improves your well-being, and sets you up for success in the demanding world of healthcare.

As we close this chapter on proactivity and resilience in healthcare, it's crucial to underscore the importance of taking personal responsibility for your well-being. The healthcare environment is fraught with stressors that can easily lead to burnout, but by being proactive and adopting healthy coping mechanisms like quality sleep and regular exercise, you're not just surviving—you're thriving. This proactive approach serves as the foundation for mastering emotional regulation, explored in the next chapter.

THE OAKLEY PARADOX: UNVEILING THE TRUTH ABOUT SELF-CARE

In the acknowledgments, I fondly referred to our Australian Shepherd, Oakley, as a calming "source of joy and relaxation." Now, it's time for a candid confession: that was an inside joke. The reality is that Oakley is anything but calm. He's a tornado of energy, highly reactive to other dogs, and can be a handful to manage when he hasn't completed fifty laps of the local field before a long rest.

Why am I revealing this now? Because Oakley's behavior serves as a poignant metaphor for the complexities of human well-being, particularly for those of us in high-stress, emotionally demanding professions like healthcare. Just like Oakley, when we neglect our own well-being—skipping exercise, cutting corners on sleep, or ignoring self-care—our behavior undergoes a noticeable shift. We become more irritable, our focus wanes, and our capacity to handle stress diminishes. Think about it. Have you ever found yourself snapping at colleagues or feeling overwhelmed by tasks that you normally handle with ease? Chances are, you were running low on self-care. It's as if we, like Oakley, start "barking" more when we're not in a good place mentally or emotionally.

So, what's the takeaway? It's simple yet profound: self-care isn't an optional indulgence; it's an essential part of being able to function at our best, both professionally and personally. And sometimes, life has a way of offering us reminders from the most unexpected quarters—like a reactive Australian Shepherd named Oakley who teaches us that taking care of ourselves is the first step in taking care of others.

Action Step: The Postal Worker Test

If you find yourself "barking" at colleagues or reacting as if every minor inconvenience is a postal worker invading your territory, it's time for a *paws*. This isn't your usual, well-trained self. It's the you who hasn't been walked, fed, or rested properly. Just like Oakley becoming a barking machine without his exercise and sleep, you too might be signaling a need for some self-care. So, if you catch yourself growling at your coworkers, consider it your inner leash tugging you towards a day off. Use it to catch up on sleep, go for a run, or simply roll over and play dead for a while. Your mental yard will be all the better for it.

CHAPTER TWO

MASTERING EMOTION REGULATION IN HEALTHCARE

UNDERSTANDING EMOTION REGULATION

EVERY DAY, healthcare professionals face an electrocardiography of emotions: from the peaks of a successful procedure to the troughs of losing a patient, roller coasting between the frustration with bureaucratic processes and the satisfaction of a grateful patient's smile.

Amidst this emotional whirlwind, maintaining equilibrium is paramount. This chapter dives into the intricacies of emotion regulation, a key resilience competency, especially vital for those in the healthcare sector.

Emotion regulation refers to the ability to effectively manage and respond to emotional experiences. Instead of suppressing feelings, it's about understanding, processing, and expressing them in an authentic and constructive manner.

Imagine a scenario where Dr. Lina, a seasoned cardiologist, loses a young patient unexpectedly. The grief is profound. Yet, in a few minutes, she has another appointment with a patient awaiting good news about his recovery. How does Dr. Lina transition between these contrasting emotions? The answer lies in effective emotion regulation.

WHY EMOTION REGULATION IS CRUCIAL IN HEALTHCARE

1. **Precise Decision-making:** Emotions can cloud judgment.

For healthcare professionals, decisions often have life-altering implications. Effective emotion regulation ensures that decisions are based on objective information and not overly influenced by transient feelings.

2. **Professional Relationships:** Interactions with peers, subordinates, and superiors are integral to healthcare. Managing emotions effectively can lead to more harmonious relationships, better teamwork, and stronger morale.

3. **Personal Well-being:** Chronic emotional turbulence can lead to burnout, anxiety, and depression. By regulating emotions, healthcare professionals can safeguard their mental health.

THE NEUROSCIENCE BEHIND EMOTION REGULATION

Our brains, especially the amygdala and the prefrontal cortex regions, play a pivotal role in emotion regulation. When we encounter emotional stimuli, the amygdala reacts instantly, triggering emotional responses. The prefrontal cortex, responsible for reasoning and decision-making, can modulate these responses.

For instance, when a patient reacts aggressively, a healthcare professional's immediate emotional response might be self-defense or retaliation. However, with effective emotion regulation, the prefrontal cortex can modulate this impulse, leading to a more measured, empathetic response.

THE STRESS-INDUCING COST OF MULTITASKING

Having explored the neuroscience behind emotion regulation, it's crucial to consider external factors that can disrupt this delicate balance. One such factor that's often overlooked is multitasking. In a high-pressure healthcare environment, multitasking might seem like a necessary skill.

However, it's worth questioning whether this juggling act is truly beneficial for your emotional well-being.

In the insightful book, *The One Thing*, by Gary Keller and Jay Papasan, multitasking is defined as **"the ability to screw up more than one thing at a time."**[5] This provocative statement invites us to reconsider the value of multitasking, especially in contexts where emotional regulation is paramount.

When you multitask, your focus is fragmented. You're not fully engaged in any of the tasks at hand, which can lead to errors. In healthcare, even a minor mistake can have life-altering implications, adding an extra layer of emotional stress. Dividing your attention can compromise your ability to regulate emotions effectively, making you more susceptible to feeling suffocated, anxious, or irritated.

As we've discussed, effective emotion regulation is crucial for patient care, professional relationships, and personal well-being. By scattering your focus, you can undermine all these aspects. So, the next time you're tempted to multitask, remember that it's not just your efficiency that's at risk—it's also your emotional equilibrium.

STRATEGIES FOR ENHANCING EMOTION REGULATION

1. **Mindful Awareness:** Being present and fully experiencing emotions without judgment can prevent impulsive reactions. Mindfulness practices, such as focused breathing or body scans, can enhance this awareness.

2. **Cognitive Reframing:** This involves changing the narrative around emotional experiences. For example, viewing challenges as opportunities for growth rather than threats.

3. **Expressive Writing:** Penning down feelings can provide clarity and serve as an emotional release. Keeping a journal can be especially therapeutic as you organize your thoughts and feelings in a logical way.

REAL-LIFE CHALLENGES IN EMOTION REGULATION

While the theoretical understanding of emotion regulation is crucial, it's equally vital to recognize the real-life challenges healthcare professionals face daily:

1. **High-Stakes Decisions:** The constant need to make decisions that can impact lives adds immense emotional pressure. A single mistake, a misjudgment, or even an unforeseen complication can result in a lifetime of guilt or regret.

2. **Difficult Patients and Families:** Interacting with aggressive, non-compliant, or overly anxious patients and their families can be emotionally draining. Balancing empathy with the need to provide effective care and maintain harmony and safety often requires immense emotional labor.

3. **Grief and Loss:** Regularly encountering death or severe illnesses can lead to accumulated grief. Many healthcare professionals, especially those in critical care or oncology, face this challenge.

4. **Workplace Dynamics:** Conflicts with peers, internal politics, or disagreements with superiors can lead to feelings of frustration or inadequacy.

ADVANCED STRATEGIES FOR EMOTION REGULATION

Having understood the challenges, let's explore advanced strategies tailored specifically for healthcare professionals:

1. **Somatic Techniques:** These involve the body in emotion regulation. Simple practices like grounding exercises, where professionals focus on physical sensations (e.g., feeling their feet on the ground), can help in managing acute emotional distress.

2. **Biofeedback:** This involves using electronic monitoring to convey information about physiological processes. By understanding their physiological responses to stress, professionals can learn to control them better.

3. **Emotional Agility:** Developed by psychologist Dr. Susan David, this approach emphasizes the ability to manage one's emotions with flexibility.[6] It involves recognizing emotions, labeling them accurately, understanding their sources, and then choosing actions aligned with one's values.

4. **Supervision and Peer Support:** Regular sessions where professionals can discuss their emotional challenges, gain perspective, and receive guidance can be invaluable. Peer support, especially from those in similar roles, offers the added benefit of shared experiences.

REAL-LIFE SCENARIOS AND SOLUTIONS

Scenario 1: The Aggressive Patient: Nurse Mike encounters a verbally aggressive patient due to pain and medication side effects. Instead of reacting defensively, Mike employs grounding exercises, takes a few deep breaths, and responds with calm assurance, managing to deescalate the situation.

Scenario 2: Grief Over a Lost Patient: Dr. Priya loses a young patient to a rare blood complication. The grief is insurmountable. Instead of suppressing her emotions, she attends a peer support session, writes about her feelings, and seeks supervision from trusted colleagues. This multi-pronged approach helps her process her grief constructively.

Scenario 3: Conflict with a Superior: Pharmacist Liam disagrees with a superior's decision. Instead of brooding over it, he practices emotional agility, recognizes his frustration, understands its source, and chooses to communicate his concerns assertively and respectfully.

NAVIGATING THE EMOTIONAL LANDSCAPE OF HEALTHCARE

In the dimly lit room of the hospital's intensive care unit, the rhythmic beeping of heart monitors creates a constant background din. Here, emotions run high. For healthcare professionals, this setting is a testament to the duality of their roles. They're both the beacons of hope and the bearers of bad news.

Sarah, a seasoned ICU nurse, recalls an evening that changed her perspective on emotion regulation. A young woman, barely in her twenties, was admitted after a severe car accident. The prognosis wasn't good. As hours morphed into days, Sarah watched the patient's family oscillate between hope and despair. One evening, as the sun cast golden hues through the window, the patient's mother approached Sarah, tears streaming down her face, seeking assurance.

Sarah knew the clinical facts, but in that moment, she also understood the weight of her words. Choosing them carefully, she combined honesty with empathy. It was a delicate dance of regulating her emotions while acknowledging the mother's pain. Her emotional intelligence had to be top notch.

THE SUBTLE ART OF EMOTIONAL BALANCE

For many in healthcare, emotion regulation doesn't involve stifling feelings but finding a balance. It's the art of feeling deeply yet not becoming consumed. It's about channeling emotions to foster genuine connections with patients while also ensuring personal well-being.

Dr. Alex, a pediatric oncologist, often shares his mantra, "Feel, but don't drown." He believes that his ability to connect emotionally with his young patients and their families is his strength. However, he's also learned the importance of boundaries. After a particularly tough day, he finds solace in music, letting melodies rinse through him, providing both comfort and release.

EMOTIONS AS TOOLS, NOT OBSTACLES

Instead of viewing emotions as hurdles, they can be seen as tools that inform, guide, and enhance the healthcare experience. A tear shed with a patient's family can build trust. A moment of shared laughter in the break room can lift spirits. By regulating emotions, healthcare professionals can ensure they're harnessing them constructively.

Sophia, a therapist working in a rehab center, often speaks about the transformative power of emotions. She recalls a session with a patient battling addiction. The patient's anger was palpable, a protective shield against vulnerability. Instead of pushing back, Sophia acknowledged the emotion, giving it time and space. This act of validation became the turning point in the patient's therapy journey.

In the realm of healthcare, where clinical knowledge meets raw human emotions, the journey of emotion regulation is continuous and evolving. It's a skill honed over time, shaped by experiences, and refined through introspection. As the chapters unfold, we'll go deeper into the mosaic of emotions, offering insights, stories, and strategies that echo the collective heartbeat of the healthcare community.

A TALE OF TWO EMOTIONS

In a bustling city hospital, two professionals stood out: Grace, an optimistic and vibrant nurse, and Ethan, a reserved and pragmatic doctor. Their approaches to emotion regulation were as distinct as night and day, yet equally effective.

Grace had a ritual. Every morning, before stepping into the chaos of the emergency ward, she'd stand by the window, watching the sunrise, letting the first rays of light caress her face. It was her way of grounding herself, preparing for the rollercoaster of emotions that each day inevitably brought. Her laughter was infectious, and patients often commented on her ability to bring sunshine even on the gloomiest days.

Ethan, on the other hand, had a different approach. He maintained a journal, meticulously jotting down his experiences and reflections after each shift. It was his way of processing emotions, ensuring they didn't accumulate and weigh him down. His calm demeanor was a rock for his colleagues, a steady presence amidst the storm.

One fateful evening, a major accident brought a flood of casualties to the hospital. The atmosphere was thick with tension, fear, and grief. Grace and Ethan, with their contrasting styles, became the anchors of their respective teams.

Grace, with her radiant energy, moved swiftly, offering words of comfort, sharing quick smiles, and infusing hope wherever she went.

Patients and their families felt seen and acknowledged, drawing strength from her warmth.

Ethan, with his methodical approach, ensured that no detail was overlooked. His journal entries that night were filled with raw emotions. He wrote about the young man who whispered a thank-you before surgery, the elderly woman who clutched his hand, searching for reassurance, and the little girl with pigtails who offered him a candy, her way of saying everything would be alright.

As dawn approached, the hospital corridors echoed with stories of despair and hope, loss and recovery. And at the heart of these stories were Grace and Ethan, emblematic of the diverse ways emotion regulation manifests in the healthcare world.

EMBRACING THE SPECTRUM OF EMOTION REGULATION

The beauty of emotion regulation lies in its diversity. There's no one-size-fits-all approach. It's a tapestry of strategies, woven together by individual experiences, beliefs, and personalities.

For some, like Grace, it's about external expression, connecting with others, and drawing energy from shared experiences. For others, like Ethan, it's an internal journey, a reflective process that offers clarity and peace.

The key is to recognize and honor one's unique emotional rhythm, to find practices that resonate, and to be open to evolving and adapting. In healthcare, where every day presents a myriad of emotions, this adaptability becomes the bedrock of resilience and effectiveness.

As weeks turned into months, the hospital corridors became witness to the dynamic between Grace and Ethan. Their contrasting styles not only complemented each other but also positively influenced the team and enriched their work environment.

On a particularly challenging day, with a ward full of patients battling a virulent flu strain, Grace found herself on the brink. The weight of so many suffering patients, combined with her personal challenges, threatened to drown her usually buoyant spirit. She felt the familiar signs of burnout creeping in, the emotional exhaustion that she had only heard about in hushed conversations among colleagues.

Ethan noticed. In his quiet, observant way, he approached her during a brief respite. "You know," he began, "sometimes, it's okay to lean on others. To share the weight." He handed her his journal and opened it to a page from the previous week. It detailed a day when he felt overwhelmed, questioning his decisions, and struggling with self-doubt.

But, as his writing revealed, he found solace in seeking support, in understanding that emotion regulation wasn't always a solitary journey.

Grace read with teary eyes as she realized she wasn't alone in her feelings. Ethan's act of vulnerability, his willingness to share his own challenges, became a turning point for her. She remembered the principles of being proactive and taking charge of her responses, as we discussed earlier. Drawing on those insights, she decided to seek support, engage in self-care activities that resonated with her, and acknowledge her emotions without judgment.

The subsequent weeks saw a transformation. Grace began attending mindfulness sessions, focusing on grounding exercises that helped her stay centered amidst the chaos. She also started journaling, inspired by Ethan, finding it therapeutic to jot down her feelings.

Ethan, influenced by Grace's vibrant energy, started participating in group therapy sessions, realizing the power of shared experiences. He even attended a workshop on emotional agility, understanding the nuances of navigating emotions with flexibility.

Their journey was a testament to the hospital staff. It showcased the importance of recognizing one's unique emotional rhythm while also being open to new strategies. This emotion regulation highlighted the significance of support, collaboration, and continuous learning.

Their story of hope and inspiration became legendary in the hospital. It served as a reminder that while the healthcare industry was fraught with challenges, the right tools and mindset could ensure you thrive.

The hospital corridors held countless stories, each room a world unto itself. But amidst these tales, the partnership between Grace and Ethan continued to draw attention. Their combined strength, stemming from their unique approaches to emotion regulation, was a source of inspiration for many.

One evening, after a particularly grueling shift, Grace and Ethan found themselves in the hospital's tranquil garden. The soft glow of the lampposts illuminated the blossoming flowers, and the gentle city hum in the distance provided a contrasting backdrop to the silence between them.

Ethan broke the quiet, "You know, Grace, our work requires us to be in the moment, to fully engage with our patients. But sometimes, I find myself lost in the 'what-ifs' and 'if onlys.'"

Grace looked at him, understanding the sentiment all too well. "It's about being proactive, isn't it? Not just reacting to situations but taking charge, understanding that we have the power to choose our responses."

Ethan nodded, recalling the principles they had both learned. "Exactly. It's about understanding that between stimulus and response, there's a space. And in that space lies our power to choose."

The duo met frequently in the garden, turning it into their sanctuary of reflection. They discussed their challenges, shared their triumphs, and delved deeper into understanding the principles that governed effective coping mechanisms.

During one of these sessions, Grace shared her experience with an extremely hostile family member of a patient. Instead of reacting defensively, she took a moment, breathed, and responded with empathy. "It was a conscious choice, Ethan. I remembered the principle of 'Begin with the End in Mind'. I visualized the outcome I wanted, which was a calm and productive conversation, and acted accordingly."

Ethan smiled, "It's amazing how these principles, when applied, can transform our interactions. Just the other day, I had a disagreement with a colleague. Instead of letting it escalate, I decided to 'Seek First to

Understand, Then to Be Understood.' I listened to his perspective, and it changed the entire dynamic."

Days rolled into weeks, and the garden meetings between Grace and Ethan became a staple. They discussed personal responsibility, managing priorities, understanding the importance of mutual benefit in interactions, and the power of synergizing with others.

Their journey involved personal growth and paved the way for others. They conducted workshops for their peers, sharing insights, experiences, and the transformative power of the principles they had embraced.

Word spread, and soon the hospital became a hub of positive change. Teams collaborated better, patient care improved, and the overall atmosphere became one of understanding, empathy, and proactive problem-solving.

Through their journey, Grace and Ethan showcased that while healthcare was inherently challenging, with the right mindset, tools, and principles, it was possible to not only navigate it effectively but also create lasting positive change.

In this dynamic and often unpredictable industry, emotional regulation stands as a beacon for professionals navigating the intricate balance between clinical responsibility and human connection. It's not merely suppressing or ignoring emotions but understanding, channeling, and leveraging them for better outcomes—for oneself, colleagues, and most importantly, patients. Grace and Ethan's journey highlighted the transformative power of being proactive, the significance of envisioning desired outcomes, and the importance of mutual understanding. These principles, rooted in timeless wisdom, offer healthcare professionals a roadmap to resilience, empathy, and effectiveness.

However, beyond the tales and anecdotes, the essence of this chapter is clear: emotion regulation is both an art and a science. It requires introspection, continuous learning, and the willingness to adapt. By embracing the principles discussed, healthcare professionals can ensure that they're not drowning in their demanding roles and are making a difference one patient, one interaction at a time.

As we venture into subsequent chapters, we'll delve deeper into practical strategies, real-world applications, and insights from various healthcare domains. The goal remains to equip healthcare professionals with the tools and knowledge to fulfill their roles with confidence, compassion, and competence.

Action Step: "Emo-Meter" Daily Debrief

As you clock out each day this week, don't just leave your scrubs at the door—leave your emotional baggage too. Take a 5-minute "Emo-Meter" check to pinpoint your day's emotional high tide. Jot it down, scribble your knee-jerk reaction, and then apply the "Three Deep Breaths Technique" from this chapter to recalibrate. Do the best you can to leave work at the door. Make it a habit, and you'll be navigating emotional whirlpools like a pro in no time.

CHAPTER THREE

THE PARADOX OF COMFORT

TODAY'S modern luxuries have brought unparalleled comfort into our lives. With advanced technology and organized systems, we've stream-lined our existence to maximize ease and minimize discomfort. But as Michael D. Easter highlights in *The Comfort Crisis*, this all-encompassing comfort might be costing us more than we realize.[7] Easter posits that our aversion to discomfort is robbing us of essential mental and physical growth experiences.

With healthcare, this principle is even more poignant. The profession is strewn with challenges, yet there's an underlying tendency to gravitate toward the familiar, the routine, the comfortable.

EMBRACING DISCOMFORT: THE PATHWAY TO MENTAL WELLNESS

The concept of seeking discomfort might seem counterintuitive. Why would anyone intentionally pursue situations that unsettle them? Yet, there's a profound connection between discomfort and mental wellness. Engaging in challenging situations can catalyze personal growth, resilience, and a deeper appreciation of life's joys.

Think about it: the most transformative moments in our lives often arise from adversity. These challenges, while initially daunting, teach us adaptability, perseverance, and the value of perspective. They sharpen our problem-solving skills and deepen our empathy. They remind us of our strengths, values, and capacity for resilience.

Many of the psychiatric patients I've worked with have experienced trauma. Instead of confronting and processing these painful memories, many sought escape, often leading to detrimental habits like substance abuse or alcoholism. Their attempts to disconnect from their pain only magnified their suffering in the long run.

As healthcare professionals, witnessing such struggles daily, we are not immune to the emotional toll. The weight of our responsibilities, combined with the emotional intensity of patient care, can bring you down. Every healthcare professional has moments that test their mettle. The turning point, when drenched in uncertainty and discomfort, often becomes the crucible of growth. They stretch our capabilities, making us more adaptable and resilient. The key lies in how we choose to cope.

Physical challenges outside of work, whether a rigorous hike, a martial arts class, or any activity that pushes our boundaries, offer a wholesome way to release pent-up stress. These pursuits not only boost our physical health but also instill a sense of accomplishment and self-worth. They serve as a tangible reminder that we can overcome adversity, building mental fortitude that transfers to our professional lives.

Drawing inspiration from Easter's work, deliberately stepping out of our comfort zones can lead to enhanced mental clarity, better physical health, and a heightened sense of well-being. For those in healthcare, this could translate to taking on challenges, participating in demanding training programs, or embracing strenuous activities outside of work. The goal isn't to overburden oneself but to foster resilience and mental fortitude.

MY PERSONAL JOURNEY TO SEEK DISCOMFORT

Burnout and stress were constant burdens during my career.

The demands of being a mental health nurse, coupled with the inherent challenges of the profession, had taken their toll. But amidst this turmoil, I found an unlikely outlet: Brazilian Jiu-Jitsu [NG1] and Muay Thai. These physically and mentally demanding martial arts propelled me into discomfort. Each session, each sparring match, was a lesson in humility, resilience, and adaptability. The mats became my battleground, where I grappled not just with training partners, but also my own limitations.

The principles of these martial arts echoed the teachings of *The Comfort Crisis*. They taught me the value of embracing discomfort, seeking challenges, and pushing my boundaries. The physical exertion was a balm to the mental fatigue, and the discipline and focus required in each session brought clarity to my professional life.

My transformative journey into martial arts wasn't just about learning techniques or improving physical fitness; it was about understanding the profound impact of embracing uncomfortable situations and seeking growth in adversity. It became a testament to the idea that sometimes stepping out of our comfort zones is the best way to find our true strengths.

Comfort, while soothing, can sometimes be a cage. For healthcare professionals, and indeed anyone looking to grow, understanding the power of discomfort can be transformative as you strive to find a delicate balance between seeking solace and pushing boundaries.

Walking into that Brazilian jiu-jitsu gym for the first time, I was buoyed by confidence. Given my size and stature, I anticipated that I would have a natural advantage, half expecting to excel and even dominate. However, that is not what transpired.

The intensity of that first class was nothing short of mind-blowing. The techniques, relentless cardio, and strategic nature of the sport were worlds apart from what I had imagined. By the end of the warm-up drills, I was already feeling the strain, questioning my stamina and endurance.

The true test came during the sparring sessions. Here I was, a newcomer with a size advantage, yet I found myself consistently outmaneuvered, outpaced, and outclassed. Seasoned practitioners, some significantly smaller than me, used technique, leverage, and strategy to dominate our sparring exchanges. It was humbling, to say the least. Every preconceived notion I had about physical dominance was turned on its head.

Beyond the physical challenge, jiu-jitsu offered something more profound: a mental sanctuary. The principles of the martial art – leverage, patience, and strategy – began to mirror my approach to the challenges at work. In the volatile and often unpredictable world of mental health nursing, where I regularly encountered aggression and hostility, the lessons from the mat bestowed a sense of confidence. The ability to remain calm under pressure, to think strategically, and to leverage situations to my advantage was enhanced by my experiences on the mat.

The paradoxical nature of this martial art – where physical exertion became a source of mental rejuvenation – was a revelation. After a grueling session on the mats, the accumulated stress from work seemed bearable. The mental clarity and focus I gained post-training were unparalleled.

Drawing from this personal experience, I realize the immense value of a physically demanding pursuit for healthcare professionals. While Brazilian Jiu-Jitsu was my chosen path, the core lesson is universal.

Engaging in rigorous physical activity serves as an outlet, a means to recharge, and a tool to build resilience. Whether it's jiu-jitsu, long-distance running, or even just a fierce workout in the garden, the physical challenges offer a unique pathway to mental and emotional well-being. For those in the healthcare profession, I can't recommend it enough. Embrace discomfort, seek challenges, and discover the transformative power these physical exertions can offer.

THE SCIENCE BEHIND DISCOMFORT AND GROWTH

Interestingly, the benefits of embracing discomfort aren't just anecdotal. Neuroscience provides compelling insights into how challenging situations can catalyze brain growth and enhance cognitive functions. When we expose ourselves to unfamiliar scenarios, our brains forge new neural pathways. This neuroplasticity, or the brain's ability to adapt and change, gets activated most effectively when we are out of our comfort zones.

For healthcare professionals, this scientific insight is particularly pertinent. Facing challenging situations and solving complex problems are part of our daily routine. But by diversifying the types of challenges we encounter—especially outside the workplace—we can stimulate our brains in unique ways, fostering creativity, problem-solving skills, and emotional intelligence.

TALES FROM ACROSS THE GLOBE: EMBRACING DISCOMFORT IN VARIOUS CULTURES

Different cultures around the world have long recognized the value of discomfort. In Japan, there's a concept called *Misogi,* a Shinto practice of purification. Traditionally, it involved standing under a freezing waterfall to cleanse oneself spiritually. The underlying belief is that enduring such extreme discomfort can lead to a clearer mind and purified spirit.

Similarly, the Nordic concept of *friluftsliv,* which translates to "open-air living," emphasizes the importance of connecting with nature, even in the harshest conditions. It's not uncommon to see Scandinavians taking icy plunges in the sea during winter or hiking across challenging terrains, emphasizing the belief that nature, in all its raw forms, offers profound therapeutic benefits.

Drawing parallels to healthcare, these cultural practices underline the universal recognition that comfort doesn't always equate to well-being. Sometimes, it's the challenges, the moments where we push our boundaries, that truly invigorate our spirit.

PRACTICAL WAYS TO SEEK DISCOMFORT IN DAILY LIFE

1. **Digital Detox:** In our screen-dominated world, taking a break from digital devices can be a significant challenge. Dedicate one day a week to stay unplugged. This exercise can be surprisingly difficult, but the mental clarity achieved is worthwhile.

2. **Travel Solo:** If possible, consider taking a solo trip.

Exploring a new place alone, without the crutch of familiarity, can be both challenging and liberating.

3. **Learn a New Skill:** Instead of pursuing something you're already good at, develop a completely new skill. The initial learning curve, mistakes, and small victories make the journey incredibly rewarding.

COLD WATER THERAPY: THE UNCONVENTIONAL COMFORT BREAKER

In recent years, the ancient practice of cold-water immersion, often referred to as cold water therapy has resurfaced and gained popularity, especially among high-performance athletes and wellness enthusiasts. What might initially seem like a torturous plunge into ice-cold water has profound implications for mental and physical well-being. Among many, cold-water immersion can help reduce stress, promote circulation, increase white blood cell production, and improve skin, lung health, and oxygenation.

The body's natural response to cold is to shiver, essentially its way of preserving core temperature. When you immerse yourself in cold water, the body undergoes a kind of shock, activating several beneficial processes. Cold exposure increases the release of norepinephrine in the brain, a hormone and neurotransmitter that's linked to mood, focus, and even pain reduction.

Furthermore, regular cold exposure can increase the body's metabolic rate, boosting the brown adipose tissue's activity, a type of fat responsible for generating heat. This not only assists in calorie burning but also plays a role in improving insulin sensitivity.

For healthcare professionals, the mental benefits of cold-water therapy might be even more intriguing than the physical outcomes. Cold-water immersion is a practice in mindfulness and resilience. When you're in icy water, the initial instinct is to panic and leap out as quickly as possible. But with time and practice, you learn to control your breath and calm your mind, akin to handling an emergency in a medical setting.

Dr. Rhonda Perciavalle Patrick, a prominent biomedical scientist, has spoken extensively about her experiments with cold showers.[8] She describes the experience as a daily confrontation with discomfort, a deliberate choice to start her day by stepping out of her comfort zone. Over time, she found this practice translated into other areas of her life, making her more resilient to stress and more focused in her work.

THE REAL-LIFE COLD PLUNGE: WIM HOF AND THE ICEMAN'S METHOD

Perhaps the most famous proponent of cold exposure is Wim Hof, aptly nicknamed "The Iceman." Hof has run marathons in the Arctic Circle, climbed Mount Kilimanjaro in shorts, and holds multiple world records for ice immersion. His 'Wim Hof Method' combines breathing exercises with regular cold exposure, and he claims it can improve everything from athletic performance to mental well-being.[9]

While Hof's feats are extreme, the underlying principle is accessible and relevant. By regularly confronting and embracing discomfort, we can train our minds and bodies to handle stress better, be more resilient, and approach challenges with a calm and focused attitude.

COLD COMFORT FOR HEALTHCARE PROFESSIONALS

For healthcare professionals, often faced with high-stress situations and the emotional toll of patient care, the practice of cold-water immersion can offer a unique form of release and rejuvenation. It's a physical challenge, but also a mental one, learning to remain calm under duress, breathe through discomfort, and reach the other side stronger and more centered.

Even if the thought of plunging into cold water sends shivers down your spine, don't dismiss the underlying principle. The essence here is to embrace discomfort as a catalyst for growth. So, find your own "cold plunge"—speaking up in a meeting, trying a new workout, or tackling a challenging project. The goal is to step out of your comfort zone in a way that resonates with you.

FEEDBACK LOOPS IN HEALTHCARE: LEARNING FROM DISCOMFORT

Every healthcare professional knows feedback is crucial. But how often do we seek feedback on our personal growth? Regularly soliciting feedback from peers, mentors, and even patients can be a daunting experience. Yet, it's these insights, especially the constructive criticisms, which propel us forward, allowing us to identify areas of improvement and enhancing our caregiving capacities. Any form of feedback should be viewed as a gift, whether or not you agree with the feedback, because it offers you an alternative perspective to reflect on and potentially use to become a better person.

DR. PAULINE CHEN AND THE ART OF DISCOMFORT

Dr. Pauline Chen, a renowned liver transplant surgeon, penned a memoir titled *Final Exam: A Surgeon's Reflections on Mortality*.[10] While the entire book is a compelling read about her experiences in the demanding world of transplant surgery, one particular incident stands out, demonstrating the profound relationship between discomfort and growth.

Early in her career, Dr. Chen was tasked with informing a patient's family about his sudden and unexpected death. The patient, a young father named James, had come in for what was considered a routine procedure. But complications arose, and despite the team's best efforts, they couldn't save him.

As a young doctor, Dr. Chen was not prepared for this.

Facing a grieving family, carrying such tragic news, and her own feelings of guilt and helplessness, were crushing her. She could have chosen to send a nurse or another doctor in her place. But she decided to face this challenge head-on.

She recalls the palpable tension in the room, the family's anxious faces, and the deafening silence that followed her words. The grief was raw and palpable. But amidst the tears and sorrow, there was a moment of profound connection. James' wife, through her tears, reached out and held Dr. Chen's hand, thanking her for doing everything she could.

That impossible moment became a turning point in Dr. Chen's career. She realized that while medical prowess and surgical skills were crucial, the ability to connect, embrace the distress of human emotions, and be truly present for her patients and their families was equally vital.

In the years that followed, Dr. Chen actively sought experiences that took her out of her clinical comfort zone. She attended therapy sessions, grief counseling, and communication workshops. She became an advocate for compassionate care within the medical community, emphasizing the importance of doctors being emotionally present and available for their patients.

Her story is a testament to the transformative power of discomfort. By choosing to face one of the most challenging situations in her career, Dr. Chen not only grew as a surgeon but also evolved as a compassionate caregiver. Her journey underscores the profound impact of seeking out and embracing discomfort, not just in healthcare but in all facets of life.

Action Step: Curveball Mastery

The next time life throws you a curveball, don't just catch it— knock it out of the park! Think of it as a VIP ticket to the School of Hard Knocks, where tuition is paid in blood and sweat, and the graduation gift is a better, more rounded version of you. Whether it's a work hurdle or a personal hiccup, remember that discomfort is the universe's personal trainer, early choices are your financial compass, and a good sweat is like a mental spa day. So, grab those growth opportunities by the horns and turn them into your personal steppingstones to greatness.

CHAPTER FOUR
EMBRACING NATURE'S HEALING

AH, the great outdoors, the world's free playground with its boundless landscapes, rugged terrains, pristine natural beauty, and an enduring allure that transcends cultural boundaries that speaks to the innermost yearnings of the human spirit. I touched on the importance of connecting with nature in the previous chapter. In this chapter, we'll find out why.

In healthcare, stress is all around you, as constant as air. Your daily routine has more ups and downs than the stock exchange. You might think binge-watching movies is the cure, but the real antidote to job fatigue, in all honesty, cannot be found in your comfy recliner; it's where your cell signal fades but your passion for life reignites.

Immersing yourself in nature is more than just a change of scenery. It's a recalibration of the senses and food for the soul. Listening to birds chirping instead of monitors beeping. Rustling leaves instead of rustling bedsheets. The hustle and bustle of hospital corridors replaced by peace and tranquility. And the vast, pale sky versus pale clinic walls.

But beyond the sensory shift, nature challenges the body and mind. A hike up a steep trail, a swim in a cold lake, or even weaving through a dense forest requires physical exertion, problem-solving, and adaptability. It's a reminder that outside the structured layers of healthcare, a wild, unpredictable realm that demands respect and engagement exists.

For many healthcare professionals, the post-work hours might feel like a time to disconnect and retreat from the world. But it's essential to realize that this is the time to truly live. To step out of the comfort zone, embrace the unpredictability of nature, and rediscover the joys of being alive. It's not only about escaping work but enriching life outside of it.

Seeking discomfort through nature is not just a leisure activity; it's a necessary counterbalance to the rigors of the healthcare profession. It's a call to healthcare professionals everywhere: don't just exist outside of work hours—live, explore, and thrive.

THE FORGOTTEN BOND BETWEEN HUMANS AND NATURE

In the vortex of modern life, amidst the concrete canopies and digital displays, it's easy to lose touch with the natural world. Yet, nature has always been a sanctuary for the human spirit. The serene landscapes, the rhythmic sounds of a babbling brook, the crunch of scrub – they all speak to a deep-seated connection we have with the natural environment. This bond, often overlooked, holds immense power for rejuvenation and healing.

As healthcare professionals working in high-stress environments, the taxing demands of the job, combined with long hours and emotional challenges, can leave us yearning for a reprieve. Nature offers this much needed escape. It provides a backdrop where our minds can unwind, our souls can refresh, and our bodies can reenergize.

Think back to a moment when you stood atop a hill, overlooking a vast green expanse, or when you walked along a beach with waves gently caressing your feet. Those tranquil moments aren't just fleeting feelings; they're glimpses into the therapeutic potential of nature. They remind us of a world beyond our workplace walls, beckoning us with the promise of peace and clarity.

Deeper into this chapter, we'll explore the ways nature influences our well-being, offering solace and strength. We'll uncover the science behind nature's therapeutic effects and provide practical strategies to integrate nature into our busy lives. For in nature, we find not just an escape, but a path to holistic healing.

NATURE-DEFICIT DISORDER: UNDERSTANDING THE MODERN DISCONNECT

In recent years, the term Nature-Deficit Disorder (NDD) has emerged and encapsulates the growing divide between humans and the natural world. Coined by author Richard Louv in his book, *Last Child in the Woods*, NDD isn't a medical diagnosis in the traditional sense.[11]

Instead, it's a descriptive term that captures the range of behavioral and emotional issues arising from our increasing alienation from nature.

NDD manifests in various ways. Some experience feelings of restlessness, while others might grapple with a nagging sense of being ungrounded or detached. Physical symptoms can include fatigue, stress, and even a weakened immune system. On an emotional level, the detachment from nature can contribute to feeling isolated and anxious and can induce mood fluctuations.

For healthcare professionals, understanding the concept of NDD is essential. Recognizing the signs and implications of this modern-day challenge can pave the way for proactive measures. By reconnecting with nature, even in small doses, we can counteract the effects of NDD and cultivate a sense of balance and well-being in our lives.

Recently, during one of my interactions with a patient, I was struck by a simple yet profound statement. The patient, institutionalized for many years due to committing a crime under the influence of a mental illness, expressed a deep yearning: "I just wish I could get out in nature."

Such sentiments, while heartrending, aren't uncommon among patients in similar situations. Institutionalization, especially for long durations, often creates an environment of forced comfort. While basic needs like meals and finances are taken care of, there's an undeniable deprivation of certain fundamental human experiences, especially exposure to nature.

However, it's essential to recognize that this disconnect isn't limited to institutionalized individuals. Healthcare professionals can also experience a similar deprivation. The demanding nature of our roles, combined with the many hours spent inside medical facilities, can lead to prolonged periods without any genuine interaction with the outdoors. Over time, this can manifest as feelings of burnout, stress, and a yearning for something intangible that seems just out of reach.

Long ago, people had a symbiotic relationship with nature that provided sustenance, wisdom, and even a sense of the divine. Fast forward to today, and it's a different story. The bustle of city life and relentless tech innovations have put a wedge between us and the great outdoors.

It's not just the physical distance or the concrete and steel barriers separating us from nature. It's also a mindset. In our quest for comfort and convenience, we've often relegated nature to a mere backdrop, something to admire from a window or during occasional vacations. This passive relationship stands in stark contrast to the active, immersive relationship our forebears shared with the environment.

For healthcare professionals, the challenge is twofold. Firstly, the nature of our job confines us to indoor spaces for extended periods, probably more than many other professions. Secondly, the emotional and physical demands can often leave us with little energy or inclination to seek out nature in our limited free time. Yet, it's precisely these challenges that make it crucial for us to prioritize re-establishing our bond with nature.

Taking a weekend trip to the countryside or visiting a park is not an adequate reconnection with nature. Changing our perspective and recognizing the profound ways in which nature impacts our mental and emotional well-being is. Simple acts, like tending to a plant, taking short walks outside during breaks, or even just sitting outdoors and observing the world around us, can make a significant difference.

Even brief interactions with nature can reduce stress, improve mood, and enhance cognitive function. For someone in the healthcare profession, these benefits aren't just personal; they directly influence the quality of care provided to patients. A mentally refreshed and emotionally balanced healthcare worker can offer a higher level of empathy, understanding, and effectiveness.

In essence, reclaiming our natural heritage is about recognizing and honoring the age-old bond between humans and the environment. It's about understanding that, irrespective of the advances we make, our well-being remains intrinsically linked to the world around us. And as healthcare professionals, this understanding can be a powerful tool, not just for our personal well-being but also for enhancing the quality of care we provide.

As the saying goes, "Nature is not a place to visit; it is home." This sentiment reflects the innate connection we share with the environment. But what exactly happens within us when we interact with nature? How does it alleviate stress, improve mood, and even bolster our cognitive abilities? Let's delve into the science behind these claims.

THE PHYSIOLOGICAL RESPONSE TO NATURE

When we immerse ourselves in nature, our bodies undergo a series of physiological changes. One of the most prominent is the reduction in the stress hormone, cortisol. A study conducted in Japan, where participants took part in 'Shinrin-yoku' or 'forest bathing', found that spending time in forests led to significantly lower cortisol levels compared to urban settings.[12] This reduction in cortisol translates to decreased stress and anxiety, promoting a feeling of relaxation and calm.

Furthermore, the presence of phytoncides—natural compounds released by trees—has been shown to boost the activity of white blood cells, enhancing our immune system's efficiency. This not only helps in warding off illness but also contributes to an overall feeling of vitality.

NEUROLOGICAL BENEFITS

Nature's impact isn't just limited to our physiological responses.

It has profound effects on our brain as well. Being in nature allows our minds to relax and rejuvenate. This natural break can lead to improved concentration, sharper cognitive functions, and increased creativity. A study showed that immersion in nature, away from multi-media and technology, enhances creative problem-solving abilities.[13]

Additionally, natural settings activate the parasympathetic nervous system, responsible for rest-and-digest functions, promoting relaxation and healing. In contrast, busy urban environments often trigger the sympathetic nervous system, leading to feelings of alertness and stress.

Emotional and Psychological Well-being

From an emotional perspective, nature offers a vast canvas for reflection and introspection. The sheer scale of natural landscapes, whether a sprawling forest, serene lake, or majestic mountain, can put our problems into perspective, making them seem less significant and more manageable.

Moreover, the beauty and unpredictability of nature stimulate feelings of awe, wonder, and gratitude. Such positive emotions have been linked to reduced rates of depression, better mood regulation, and higher levels of life satisfaction.

PRACTICAL STRATEGIES FOR HEALTHCARE PROFESSIONALS

Understanding the science behind nature's therapeutic effects is enlightening, but the key lies in its application. For healthcare professionals, who grapple with demanding schedules and emotionally taxing situations, integrating nature into daily routines becomes paramount.

1. **Micro-breaks with Nature:** Even if it's just a few minutes, taking short breaks to step outside can be rejuvenating. Whether it's observing the shapes of leaves, listening to bird songs, or simply feeling the sun on your skin, these brief moments can have a cumulative positive effect.

2. **Indoor Plants:** Bringing nature indoors is a feasible solution for those who can't step out frequently. Tending to a plant, watching it grow, and being in its presence can offer the many benefits associated with being outdoors.

3. **Mindful Nature Walks:** Once a week, consider taking a mindful walk in a natural setting. This isn't about exercise but about truly immersing oneself in the environment. Feel the ground beneath your feet while listening to the symphony of sounds and let nature's essence permeate your being.

THERAPEUTIC BREAKS IN NATURAL SETTINGS

More and more healthcare institutions recognize the importance of providing their staff with access to natural spaces. These therapeutic landscapes or gardens within hospital premises serve as sanctuaries for staff to de-stress and rejuvenate.

Imagine a brief break where one can step out and be enveloped in the fragrance of flowers, the gentle hum of bees, or the soothing sound of water. These sensory experiences can offer a quick mental reset, preparing healthcare professionals for the challenges ahead.

ENGAGING IN NATURE-BASED ACTIVITIES

1. **Gardening and Horticulture:** Even a small act, like tending to a plant in one's office or home, can be a source of relaxation. The act of nurturing something, watching it grow, can provide a sense of accomplishment and a break from routine stresses.

2. **Nature Walks and Hikes:** Regular walks in a park, forest, or beach can be therapeutic. Physical activity, combined with the serene surroundings, can be a potent combination to combat stress and mental fatigue.

3. **Nature Art and Craft:** Engaging in art and craft using natural materials can be both a creative outlet and a way to connect with nature. It offers a break from the digital world and a chance to create something tangible.

DIGITAL DETOX THROUGH NATURE

While the digital age offers many obvious conveniences, it also brings a barrage of information and a constant state of connectivity. For healthcare professionals, who often need to be on call or accessible, this can add to the mental load. Periodic digital detoxes, where one disconnects from electronic devices and immerses oneself in nature, can be highly beneficial. This could be a simple evening without screen time, spent in the backyard, or a weekend getaway to a natural haven.

ADVOCATING FOR NATURE-INCLUSIVE WORKSPACES

It's crucial for healthcare professionals to voice the need for nature-inclusive spaces in their work environment such as small gardens, indoor plants in common areas, or even nature-themed relaxation rooms.

Furthermore, professionals can also seek out workshops or courses that cover the therapeutic aspects of nature. Knowledge gained can be shared with peers, amplifying the benefits across the board.

For healthcare professionals, nature isn't just a luxury; it's a necessity. It offers a refuge from the demanding nature of their roles. By embracing nature, they find not just relaxation but also the strength to continue their life-saving work with renewed vigor.

Action Step: Nature's Fix

Steal a few minutes from your hectic schedule for a rendezvous with the outdoors. Step outside and let your senses off the leash. Listen to the birds, enjoy the breeze, or simply become a nature detective, spotting the colors and designs that only the outdoors can offer. Consider it a mental espresso shot, dialing down stress and tuning up your focus for the next healthcare hurdle.

CHAPTER FIVE
FINANCIAL WELL-BEING AND MENTAL HEALTH

THE FINANCIAL COMFORT TRAP: A CALL TO HEALTHCARE PROFESSIONALS

IN A FIELD DEVOTED to mending bodies and minds, it's a cruel twist of fate that many healthcare professionals find themselves in financial triage. Sure, the high-profile job is often seen as a golden ticket—especially for high-earning specialists like surgeons. But the truth is, many are more financially insecure than they'd care to admit.

After years of academic study, many graduates cross the finish line only to be greeted by a mountain of student loan debt. But the real kicker? The post-grad spending bonanza. Blame it on the shiny new paycheck, but too many fall prey to the siren call of luxury cars, fancy homes, and Instagram-worthy getaways. Welcome to the "Financial Mirage"—that deceptive oasis where you think you can afford more than you actually can.

Yet, the advice for healthcare professionals should be no different from anyone else: the early years in one's career are crucial for setting a solid financial foundation. It's a time to prioritize savings, investments, and, most importantly, stay out of debt. In the words of personal finance guru Dave Ramsey, "Live like no one else, so that later, you can live and give like no one else."[14] This mantra underscores the importance of short-term sacrifices for long-term benefits.

Central to this philosophy is the concept of an emergency fund—a financial buffer to handle unexpected expenses. For healthcare professionals, the stakes are even higher. The daily stresses of patient care, long hours, and the emotional toll of the profession are burdensome enough. Add financial worries to the mix, and it's a recipe for burnout.

A fully funded emergency fund of three to six months of expenses serves multiple purposes. On a practical level, it ensures that unexpected expenses, whether medical emergencies, car repairs, or a leaking roof, don't lead to debt. But perhaps even more importantly, it provides invaluable psychological peace of mind. Knowing there's a safety net can make all the difference in how one approaches challenges. As mentioned, with an emergency fund in place, a sudden expense becomes an inconvenience, not a crisis.

Healthcare professionals, with their unique set of challenges and responsibilities, cannot afford to fall into the financial comfort trap. The profession demands mind clarity, focus, and emotional stability. And while money can't buy happiness, sound financial practices can undoubtedly provide peace, security, and the freedom to focus on what truly matters: spending time with loved ones.

THE POWER OF DEBT-FREE LIVING AND SMARTER FINANCIAL CHOICES

One of the most destructive forms of stress for many individuals, regardless of profession, is financial. The weight of debt, with its accumulating interest and the constant pressure to make repayments, can be suffocating. For healthcare professionals, already bearing the substantial emotional and physical demands of their roles, adding financial worries to the mix can prove the final straw.

Being free from the burden of debt is not merely having more disposable income; it's about liberating the mind. Without looming repayments, one can approach life with a sense of freedom, security, and possibility. Decisions are no longer dictated by financial constraints but are instead guided by genuine desires, ambitions, and needs.

But how does one achieve this coveted debt-free ideal? A key strategy is prevention—avoiding debt in the first place. While certain debts, such as student loans, might be difficult to avoid completely, consumer debts, especially those related to lifestyle choices, are preventable.

Take, for instance, the common aspiration to own a brand-new car. While the allure of a shiny, untouched vehicle is undeniable, it's essential to consider the financial implications. Vehicles are notorious for their rapid depreciation, with the most significant loss in value occurring within the first two years. This means the moment you drive a brand-new car off the dealership lot, it instantly loses a significant portion of its worth. It's akin to burning a chunk of hard-earned money with a lighter.

A smarter financial move would be to consider purchasing a reliable vehicle at least two years old. Not only does this shield you from the steepest depreciation curve, but it also often means a lower purchase price, reduced insurance costs, and, in many cases, the same modern amenities and safety features of newer models. It's a choice that combines practicality with financial prudence. As an added bonus, cars with a track record for dependability often retain their value far better than their high-end, luxury counterparts.

Therefore, the path to financial well-being and reduced stress is paved with informed decisions. By understanding the true cost of debt, recognizing its implications on mental and emotional well-being, and proactively making choices that prevent unnecessary financial burdens, healthcare professionals can cultivate a life where their primary focus remains on their passion: healing and caring for others, unencumbered by avoidable financial worries. There will be room to enjoy your money later on, if you sacrifice and make smart financial choices from the outset.

A TALE OF TWO NURSES

Jane and Sarah, both fresh out of nursing school, landed jobs at the same hospital with an $80,000 starting salary. But their financial decisions set them on two immensely different paths.

Jane bought a house with an extra living space downstairs. She rented it out to travel nurses for $1,500 a month and increased the monthly rent by $50 each year. Instead of spending this extra income, she invested it in an S&P 500 index fund, known for its 7% average annual return. Three years later, she turned her entire home into a rental property, purchased a new home to move into, and used the rental income from her first home to save up for a downpayment to do it all over again.

Sarah, on the other hand, celebrated her new job by buying a luxury house and car. Her monthly bills ate most of her salary, leaving her with little to no savings or investments. She could rarely afford a much-needed vacation, away from the pressures of healthcare.

Fast forward 30 years. Jane's smart investments and rental income have grown her net worth to an impressive $4 million. Her property is paid off, and she continues to earn rental income. Sarah's net worth is around $600,000, mostly tied up in her home's value. While it sounds like a lot, it won't support the lifestyle she's accustomed to in retirement. She now faces a tough choice: work past retirement age or cut back on spending, notably more difficult after years of living large.

The takeaway? Early career choices can make or break your financial future. Choose wisely.

THE POWER OF EARLY CHOICES

Jane's story highlights the transformative power of early financial decisions. Her initial sacrifices and wise investments not only allowed her to amass considerable wealth but also offered her the luxury of choice. With her significant net worth, Jane could opt for early retirement if she wished, transitioning into a life of leisure or pursuing passions outside of her nursing career.

Sarah, while enjoying her early years of luxury, found herself without the vast reserves of wealth or the financial freedom that Jane enjoyed. Her choices, while gratifying in the moment, lacked long-term vision. She remained independent on an income from her employer for much longer than she would have liked; she had no other choice.

This tale underscores a timeless financial lesson: the choices we make early on have long-lasting ramifications. While both nurses lived fulfilling lives, Jane's early sacrifices and prudent decisions set her up for financial independence, offering her the possibility of an early retirement—a dream many aspire to, but few achieve.

FINANCIAL STRESS: THE SILENT STRAIN ON HEALTHCARE PROFESSIONALS

Hospital corridors and clinics often resonate with beeping monitors, families' hushed conversations, and the marching steps by doctors and nurses attending to their patients. What you don't hear are the alarm bells of financial stress on healthcare professionals.

Melissa, a pediatric nurse with a decade of experience, often found herself lying awake at night, not because of work matters but because of her mounting credit card bills. With two children and a mortgage, she struggled to keep up with her expenses, despite earning a decent salary. The constant worry about making ends meet took a toll on her mental well-being, affecting her performance at work. She was not alone in her struggles. Many of her colleagues, despite their seemingly comfortable lifestyles, were facing similar challenges.

Financial stress is pervasive, casting a shadow over every decision and interaction. For healthcare professionals, already navigating the complexities of patient care, this added layer of stress is one more they could really do without.

It creates the sense of feeling trapped, the fear of unforeseen expenses, and the pressure to maintain a certain lifestyle. This is especially true for younger professionals, fresh out of medical school or nursing programs, juggling student loan repayments with the costs of starting a family or buying a home.

Dr. Rajesh, a cardiologist, highlighted a profound observation: "In the ER, we're trained to recognize the signs of a heart attack, but no one teaches us to recognize the signs of financial distress in ourselves or our colleagues. And yet, it affects our well-being just as critically."

BUDGETING, SAVING, AND INVESTING: TOOLS FOR FINANCIAL WELLNESS

The journey to financial wellness begins with understanding one's finances. It sounds simple, yet many avoid looking at their bank statements or setting a budget, fearing what they might find. But avoidance only amplifies the problem.

1. **Budgeting**: The first step is to establish a clear budget. Knowing where your money is going and making informed decisions can only lead to good outcomes. Tools like mobile apps or spreadsheets can help track expenses and set limits. For healthcare professionals with hectic schedules, setting aside a dedicated time each month to review finances can make all the difference.

2. **Saving**: Once a budget is in place, the next step is to prioritize savings. Even if it's a small amount initially, the act of saving can provide a sense of control and security. An emergency fund, as previously discussed, is essential. Beyond that, saving for important goals such as a new car or retirement can provide direction and motivation.

3. **Investing**: With savings in place, investment opportunities arise. While it might seem daunting, especially with the range of options available, starting with basic investment vehicles like a 401(k) or an IRA can set the foundation. For those unsure of where to begin, consult with a fee only financial advisor. First, start reading and educate your-

self about finances. Look for my recommended list of books in the resources page on my website: www.self-care-rx.com

Financial literacy is not just about understanding money; it's about empowerment. It's the tool that allows healthcare professionals to focus on their primary mission of caring for others without a constant financial burden.

THE ROLE OF FINANCIAL LITERACY IN PREVENTING BURNOUT

Burnout is a real and pressing concern in the healthcare industry. Long hours, emotional challenges, and heavy responsibility can lead to exhaustion and disillusionment. Sprinkling some financial stress into this mix can be the tipping point.

Educating oneself about financial matters, seeking advice when needed, and being proactive about money can alleviate a significant portion of this stress. Institutions, recognizing this link, are increasingly offering financial wellness programs as part of their employee benefits.

Anna, a respiratory therapist, shared her transformative experience after attending a financial literacy workshop organized by her hospital. "I realized I wasn't alone in my struggles," she reflected. "The workshop gave me the tools and confidence to take charge of my finances. It was as if a weight had been lifted."

While the healthcare profession is undoubtedly demanding, financial stress need not be an added burden. With the right tools, knowledge, and support, financial well-being is within reach, paving the way for a more balanced and fulfilling professional journey.

THE RELATIONSHIP BETWEEN FINANCIAL HEALTH AND PHYSICAL WELL-BEING

In the sprawling campus of St. John's Medical Center, Dr. Elizabeth Green, a seasoned endocrinologist, often noticed a curious pattern among her colleagues. Those who frequently discussed or exhibited signs of financial stress, whether lamenting about loans or their children's education costs, often exhibited physical symptoms of stress too. From recurrent headaches to a compromised immune system leading to frequent colds, the connection between financial woes and physical ailments became increasingly clear to Dr. Green.

The science behind this observation is not new. Financial stress, like other forms of stress, triggers the body's "fight or flight" response, leading to the release of stress hormones like cortisol. Elevated cortisol levels, especially if sustained over time, have been linked to multiple health issues, from weight gain and digestive problems to chronic conditions like heart disease and diabetes.[15]

For healthcare professionals, this is particularly concerning. A nurse or doctor already has a demanding job that requires them to be in optimal health. Adding financial stress to the equation not only compromises their well-being but can also affect the quality of care they provide to their patients.

MINDFULNESS AND FINANCIAL DECISIONS: THE INTERTWINING PATHS

Mindfulness, a concept rooted in ancient Eastern philosophies, has gained significant traction in the West, especially where mental health and personal well-being are concerned. At its core, mindfulness involves being present and acutely aware of one's surroundings, emotions, and thoughts without being judgmental.

But how does this relate to financial well-being?

When applied to financial decisions, mindfulness encourages an acute awareness of one's financial habits. It prompts individuals to pause and reflect before making impulsive purchases, understand the emotional triggers behind certain financial behaviors, and recognize patterns that might be detrimental in the long run.

Dr. Laura Simmons, a psychologist specializing in behavioral therapy, started incorporating financial mindfulness into her sessions after noticing the profound impact of financial stress on her patients, of whom many were fellow healthcare professionals. Through guided exercises, she helped her patients visualize their financial goals, understand their spending triggers, and cultivate a more mindful approach to money.

The results were transformative. Many reported not only an improvement in their financial health but also a decrease in anxiety and a heightened sense of overall well-being. The exercise of financial mindfulness, while simple in its approach, transcended in multiple facets of their lives.

COMMUNITY AND COLLECTIVE FINANCIAL WELLNESS

One of the most influential tools in promoting financial wellness is community. Sharing financial challenges, successes, and strategies among peers can be both therapeutic and educational. Recognizing this, many healthcare institutions are fostering financial support groups or workshops, allowing professionals to come together and learn from one another.

Alexandra, a surgical nurse, was initially hesitant to join one such group at her hospital. Discussing finances, she felt, was deeply personal. After attending a few sessions, her perspective shifted. She found solace in knowing she wasn't alone in her financial struggles and was invigorated by the collective brainstorming on tackling common financial challenges.

These community-driven initiatives are creating a cultural shift, breaking the taboo around discussing money and promoting a collective journey toward financial well-being. As professionals band together, sharing resources, strategies, and experiences, the path to financial wellness becomes less daunting and more achievable.

Whether discussing financial, mental, or physical well-being, it once again highlights the importance of sharing and collaboration.

Inherently, while the healthcare industry is fraught with challenges, financial stress can be eliminated. By integrating mindfulness, community support, and a proactive approach to money, healthcare professionals can chart a path to financial wellness, ensuring they remain at he top of their mental and physical game, as they continue their instrumental work of healing and care.

NAVIGATING STUDENT LOANS AND OTHER DEBTS: A CAUTIONARY TALE FOR HEALTHCARE PROFESSIONALS

Medical institutions are often abuzz with tales of lucrative prospects that await healthcare graduates. The allure of a financially prosperous life becomes the beacon for many during their rigorous academic journey. However, overshadowing these dreams is an often-underestimated specter: the formidable student loans and the potential long-term ramifications they present.

For numerous healthcare professionals, student loans appear as a necessary passage to realize their career dreams. But it's of utmost importance to tread this path with a clear understanding of its long-erm implications. Let's explore the strategies for managing, minimizing, and, if possible, sidestepping these debts, to ensure they don't impinge upon the emotional and mental wellness of our devoted healthcare practitioners.

THE SILENT STRESSOR: THE PSYCHOLOGICAL IMPACT OF DEBT

Take the instance of Dr. Hannah, a pediatrician in her early 30s. She often refers to her $200,000 student loan as an unshakable shadow that constantly looms large. A significant portion of her paycheck is regularly siphoned off toward loan repayments, instilling feelings of perpetual financial entrapment. Such sentiments echo among many healthcare professionals.

Despite earning respectable salaries, the relentless debt repayment cycle can induce feelings of professional burnout, reduced job satisfaction, and even second thoughts about their chosen career path.

MINIMIZE TO MAXIMIZE: THE MANTRA FOR STUDENT LOANS

While the pursuit of knowledge is noble, diving headlong into massive debt based on anticipated future earnings is a precarious venture.

Remember, while the end of one's educational endeavors isn't set in stone, the commitment to repay borrowed amounts is unwavering. Even in the face of unforeseen challenges or personal bankruptcies, student loans persist. Loan forgiveness, especially during political campaigns, may seem promising but often remains an elusive dream.

The guiding principle for aspiring healthcare professionals is lucid: keep student loans to an absolute bare minimum. This could involve choosing educational institutions that offer more economical tuition fees, actively seeking out scholarships, or taking on part-time jobs to alleviate some of the educational expenses. The initial financial prudence can set the stage for a future free from monumental loan repayments.

A PRACTICAL APPROACH: TACKLING AND CLEARING DEBTS

While student loans are often the focal point, they're not the only financial obligations many grapple with. Credit card debt, mortgages, and car loans can also stack up. Here, the debt snowball method shines. By concentrating on clearing smaller debts first, individuals experience psychological wins, fostering motivation to tackle larger debts. This approach, while not always mathematically optimal like the debt avalanche method, harnesses the power of positive psychological reinforcement, making the journey of debt clearance feel more achievable and less daunting.

BEYOND DEBT: THE IMPERATIVE OF FINANCIAL LITERACY

This discussion, although emphasizing the paramount importance of curtailing student loans, is but a fragment of the broader financial wellness narrative. Dedicate time to grasp the basics of personal finance, from judicious budgeting to informed investing, to lay the groundwork for a robust financial future.

Debt, especially student loans, might feel like an inevitable part of a healthcare professional's journey. However, with strategic planning, foresight, and proactive steps, it's possible to minimize, and in some cases prevent this burden. As we traverse the complex terrains of financial obligations, one crucial aspect often remains uncharted, yet it holds the key to long-term financial well-being and emotional stability: financial literacy.

Action Step: Knock out Debt

Take a moment this week to assess your current debts, listing them from smallest to largest. Choose the smallest debt and set a tangible goal to clear it using the debt snowball method. As you make progress, observe the psychological relief it brings. This small step not only sets you on a path towards financial freedom but also aids in reducing potential stressors that contribute to burnout. Embrace the empowerment that comes from taking control of your financial well-being.

CHAPTER SIX
ENGAGING IN AUTHENTIC HUMAN CONNECTION

IN TODAY'S digitally driven age, there's an irony we can't ignore; while technology has given us tools to connect more than ever, feelings of isolation, loneliness, and detachment are on the rise. For healthcare professionals, especially those working long shifts and irregular hours, it's not uncommon to fall into patterns of isolation outside of work, further compounding the stress and burnout of their profession.

In the hospital setting, interactions often revolve around clinical procedures, updates, and emergencies. The focus is, rightly so, on the patients and their well-being. But outside of these interactions, the personal connections between colleagues can sometimes feel superficial, limited to quick greetings or brief exchanges about the weather or weekend plans.

Yet, these very connections, when deepened, can be a source of immense comfort and strength. Engaging in genuine human connection with colleagues, friends, or family, can serve as a buffer against the mental and emotional challenges of the medical profession. Laughter, shared stories, a random joke, or crude comment are moments that help ground us, reminding us of our shared humanity. These authentic interactions are often lacking in our busy lives.

Consider that after a particularly challenging day at the hospital, instead of retreating to solitude or losing oneself in digital distractions, what if you reached out? A simple call to a friend, joining a community group, or even spending quality time with family can make a world of difference.

Research shows that social connections can boost mental health, reduce stress levels, and even increase lifespan. Dr. Julianne Holt-Lunstad, a psychologist at Brigham Young University, found that social connections not only impact mental well-being but also have tangible effects on physical health, reducing the risk of chronic diseases, and even enhancing longevity.[16]

For healthcare professionals, taking the time to nurture these relationships outside of work becomes even more crucial. The support system they create can serve as an anchor, helping them navigate the turbulent waters of their profession.

While immediate comfort might tempt one to remain isolated, it's essential to recognize the long-term benefits of forging authentic human connections. Like muscles that need regular exercise to remain strong, our social connections need consistent engagement to thrive. In seeking discomfort by stepping out of our comfort zones to connect with others, we're not only enhancing our mental well-being but also fortifying ourselves against the unique challenges of the healthcare profession.

Our work is filled with moments that test our mettle, challenge our beliefs, and stretch our emotional boundaries. These experiences, both uplifting and heart-wrenching, form the tapestry of a healthcare professional's journey. Yet, it's the shared experiences and the moments we open up to allow others in that often have the most profound impact on our well-being.

It's no surprise that many healthcare professionals form tight-knit bonds with their colleagues. The long hours, shared patients, collective victories, and losses create a bond that's hard to replicate in other settings. However, to truly harness the power of these shared experiences, one must be willing to venture beyond the superficial.

While the practice of medicine often requires an analytical, data-driven approach, it's essential not to lose sight of the human element.

Communicating on a more personal level, whether discussing a challenging case with a colleague, debriefing after a particularly grueling shift, or even sharing a light-hearted moment during a coffee break, helps break down barriers and foster a sense of belonging.

Moreover, sharing experiences isn't limited to colleagues.

Engaging in community activities, participating in support groups, or even joining a book club can provide avenues to connect with diverse groups of people. Each interaction enriches our understanding of the world and fortifies our mental well-being.

Regarding mental health, the act of sharing is therapeutic. It validates feelings, offers perspectives, and provides a safe space to process emotions. For healthcare professionals, the act of sharing is not just therapeutic; it's essential. It's a bridge that connects the clinical with the personal, the analytical with the emotional.

As we continue our journey through the terrain of discomfort, we must remember that while the path can sometimes be solitary, the experiences are meant to be shared. In doing so, we not only heal ourselves but also strengthen the bonds that tie us to our community.

In healthcare, it's easy to let one's professional life become the epicenter of their existence. The long hours, emotional investment in patients, and camaraderie with colleagues can sometimes blur the lines between work and personal life.

One of the challenges many face in today's digital connectivity age is the paradox of feeling isolated despite being more 'connected' than ever. Social media platforms, while valuable for staying in touch, often offer a curated version of reality, leading to feelings of inadequacy and loneliness. Moreover, as adults, the avenues for making new friends become limited, with many lamenting the difficulty of forming genuine connections post-college.

Yet, the importance of having a social circle outside of work cannot be overstated. These relationships allow us to step back, gain perspective, and mentally detach from the challenges of our profession. They provide a safe space where we can be ourselves without looming work-related stressors. Engaging with friends who aren't privy to the intricacies of our profession offers a refreshing change of pace, allowing us to discuss topics and indulge in activities that don't revolve around our work.

So, how does one go about forging these connections in adulthood, especially in an era dominated by virtual interactions?

The answer lies in shared interests. Joining groups or clubs centered around hobbies or passions can be a fantastic way to meet like-minded individuals. Whether it's a book club, a hiking group, a community theater, or a martial arts class, these gatherings offer a dual benefit.

They provide an avenue to pursue personal interests while also facilitating organic, meaningful interactions.

For healthcare professionals, this approach can be particularly therapeutic. After a grueling shift, attending a yoga class or photography workshop not only serves as a mental diversion but also incorporates the added benefit of physical activity. Engaging the body and mind in tandem can be incredibly rejuvenating, helping to mitigate the effects of work-related stress.

Furthermore, these group activities often lead to friendships that are rooted in mutual interests, making them more likely to stand the test of time. As is often experienced with Brazilian Jiu-Jitsu, the shared struggles, triumphs, and vulnerability foster a bond that goes beyond mere acquaintance.

While the bonds formed at work are important, it's essential to maintain a balance. Cultivating relationships outside of the workplace, grounded in shared interests and activities, not only enriches our personal lives but also provides the mental fortitude needed to face the challenges of our profession with resilience and grace.

MEANINGFUL RELATIONSHIPS: BUILDING BRIDGES IN AND OUT OF THE HOSPITAL

Relationships, both within and outside the workplace, play a pivotal role in a healthcare professional's well-being.

1. Fostering Team Spirit: A hospital or clinic is a mosaic of different professionals, each playing a crucial role. Building relationships with colleagues, understanding their strengths and challenges, and appreciating their contributions to the team and the profession can foster a more harmonious work environment for all.

2. Mentor-Mentee Bonds: The medical field, with its vast knowledge base and numerous skilled professionals, is ripe for mentorship opportunities. These relationships can be immensely rewarding, offering guidance to the mentee and a sense of fulfillment to the mentor.

3. Digital Detox: In today's connected world, it's easy to feel overwhelmed by the constant barrage of information and misinformation, and the relentless ping of notifications. Setting aside dedicated 'digital detox' time can help foster genuine, face-to-face connections.

4. Shared Experiences: Engaging in activities that resonate personally, like group fitness classes, book clubs, or cooking classes, can help forge deep, meaningful relationships based on shared interests.

While the healthcare profession is undoubtedly demanding, it's these meaningful work experiences and relationships that make the journey worthwhile. They serve as anchors, providing stability in the face of challenges and enriching the professional journey with personal growth and fulfillment.

BALANCING PROFESSIONAL AND PERSONAL: THE NEED FOR EXTERNAL CONNECTIONS

Achieving a work-life balance in healthcare often seems like an elusive dream. The lines between professional responsibilities and personal life blur, making it challenging to switch off from work mode and fully engage in personal experiences. The result? A constant state of mental fatigue, reduced personal engagements, and an increased sense of professional burnout.

Consider the story of Dr. Richard, a seasoned cardiologist known for his dedication and commitment. Over the years, his work became his identity. He was often the first to arrive at the hospital and the last to leave. Weekends were mostly spent catching up on medical journals or preparing for conferences. While his professional accolades grew, his personal life took a backseat. Friends, hobbies, and family gatherings became rare occurrences. Over time, the lack of personal connections began to weigh on him, leading to feelings of loneliness and detachment. He began to question the very essence of his professional journey.

One evening, after a particularly challenging day at the hospital, Dr. Richard stumbled upon a local community event while taking a walk. On a whim, he decided to attend. The event was a celebration of local art and culture, featuring music, dance, and storytelling sessions. As he immersed himself in the activities, he felt a sense of liberation he hadn't experienced in years. Conversations flowed freely, laughter echoed, and for the first time in a long while, Dr. Richard felt genuinely connected.

This serendipitous evening became a turning point for him. He realized the importance of forging connections outside his professional scene. Dr. Richard began to actively seek out community events, reconnected with old friends, and even took up painting. The change was palpable. Not only did he feel more rejuvenated and content in his personal life, but his professional interactions also became more empathetic and compassionate. The balance he achieved acted as a protective barrier against the stresses of his demanding profession.

Dr. Richard's story underscores a vital lesson for healthcare professionals: while dedication to one's profession is commendable, it's essential to carve out time for personal engagements. These external connections act as a counterbalance, providing much-needed respite from the relentless demands of the healthcare industry.

In summary, moments of genuine human connection, both within and outside the healthcare profession, bring balance and purpose, reminding us of the broader tapestry of life. By actively nurturing these connections, healthcare professionals can ensure not just professional excellence but also personal fulfillment and well-being.

ADULT FRIENDSHIPS IN A DIGITAL WORLD: BEYOND THE SCREEN TO GENUINE BONDS

For many, forging friendships during school and college days is a vivid memory—shared classes, group projects, dormitory life, and extracurricular activities provided ample opportunities to bond. Yet, in adulthood, the dynamics of friendship change. For healthcare professionals, the challenge of building and maintaining adult friendships becomes even more pronounced.

Nowadays, while our smartphones draw us in with notifications from various social media platforms, genuine connection can feel elusive. The paradox is clear: in an era of unprecedented connectivity, many feel more isolated than ever. But why?

The digital realm, while offering numerous advantages, often presents a curated version of reality. Endless streams of perfectly posed photos, celebratory life updates, and highlight reels can unintentionally foster feelings of inadequacy, leading many to question their own life choices, especially when they are already under work stress.

However, the solution isn't to abandon the digital world but to use it with intention and purpose. Here's how healthcare professionals can leverage digital devices to foster genuine bonds:

1. **Move Beyond the Screen:** Social media platforms can be a starting point, not the destination. Join online groups and forums related to your interests. These can be medical discussions, hobbies, or book clubs. Engage in meaningful conversations, and when comfortable, transition these online interactions to real-life meetups. Platforms like Meetup.com offer an array of groups based on shared interests and can be a goldmine for professionals looking to connect outside of their work environment.

2. **Shared Interests as a Catalyst:** Shared activities provide a natural setting for genuine interactions. Whether it's a pottery class, community garden project, or local choir group, such avenues allow for repeated, informal interactions, laying the foundation for deeper connections. For a healthcare professional, joining a yoga or meditation group can offer the dual benefit of relaxation and potential friendships.

3. **Workshops and Conferences:** For healthcare professionals, attending workshops, seminars, and conferences can serve a dual purpose. While they offer opportunities for professional growth, they also provide a platform to meet like-minded individuals, paving the way for both collaborations and friendships.

4. **Reconnect with Old Friends:** While forging new bonds is essential, revisiting old friendships can be equally rewarding. With platforms like LinkedIn or alumni networks, reconnecting has never been easier. A simple message can rekindle a lost bond, providing a sense of familiarity and comfort as you journey down memory lane.

5. **Volunteer:** Offering one's skills and time for a cause can be deeply fulfilling. For healthcare professionals, medical camps, community health drives, or even mentoring programs can be avenues where professional skills align with personal passions. Such endeavors not only offer personal satisfaction but also provide opportunities to connect with individuals from diverse backgrounds, united by a shared purpose.

At heart, while the challenges of adult friendships in the digital age are real, they're not insurmountable. With intentionality, openness, and a bit of effort, healthcare professionals can cultivate a vibrant social circle that complements their demanding professional life. As they master the art of building genuine personal relationships, they are better equipped to deal with the complex dynamics of patient relationships, the focus of our next chapter. Just as personal connections provide solace and rejuvenation, understanding and effectively managing patient relationships can be the key to a fulfilling and balanced professional journey.

Action Step: Connection Hour

Set aside one hour a week for real face-to-face connection. Use this time to call an old friend, join a local group, or have quality family time without distractions. Make this hour a fixed part of your week. This simple step can help you build stronger relationships and cope better with the stresses of your job.

CHAPTER SEVEN

WEATHERING THE STORM: STRATEGIES FOR DEALING WITH DIFFICULT PATIENTS AND FAMILIES

IN THE CHALLENGING but rewarding field of psychiatric nursing, every day brings new opportunities for both personal and professional growth. As we navigate the complexity of mental healthcare, we inevitably cross paths with a variety of individuals with their own unique needs, histories, and behavior patterns.

It's not uncommon to encounter a particularly difficult patient who demands an extra measure of patience, skill, and emotional resilience. Just when you think you've scaled that mountain, you may find yourself meeting the patient's family members—often parents—who present challenges equal to, if not exceeding, those posed by the patient themselves.

Why does this phenomenon occur, and how does it impact our role as psychiatric nurses? Is there a pattern to the difficulties we face, and more importantly, are there effective strategies we can employ to handle these stormy waters? As mental health professionals, our primary goals are to provide the best possible care for our patients while maintaining a level of self-care that allows us to perform our duties sustainably. However, achieving these goals becomes increasingly complex when dealing with difficult patients and families.

This chapter explores the intricacies of managing such challenging interactions, the psychology behind difficult behaviors, present proven methods for de-escalation, and guidelines for setting specialized boundaries that protect both you and your patient. Further, we'll discuss team-based approaches for managing these complexities and address the all-important aspects of self-care and emotional resilience, especially vital in these situations.

Through an understanding of the underlying dynamics and equipped with a set of practical tools, you'll be better prepared to deal with these challenges, not just as obstacles but as opportunities for growth and improvement in your practice.

Difficult patient and family interactions are an integral part of the mental health nursing journey. Consider this chapter your navigational chart, designed to guide you safely through the tempests you'll encounter along the way.

With this foundation laid, let's delve into the strategies and insights that can help you sail through these turbulent waters with confidence and skill.

RECOGNIZING DIFFICULT BEHAVIOR

In psychiatric nursing, where complex emotional and psychological factors come into play, recognizing difficult behavior may often extend beyond the obvious signs of confrontation or non-compliance. The challenge often lies in discerning patterns, subtleties, and nuances that can inform a more comprehensive understanding of the patient and their family dynamics.

BEYOND THE OBVIOUS: UNPACKING BEHAVIORAL PATTERNS

Patients who pose challenges are not always overtly confrontational or openly non-compliant. Sometimes, the issues are subtler but can be just as disruptive to effective treatment. For instance:

1. **Manipulative Behavior:** Some patients might try to pit staff members against each other to create internal conflicts that distract from their own non-compliance or maladaptive behaviors.

2. **Covert Non-Compliance:** There may be patients who seemingly agree with the treatment plan in your presence but have no intention of following through, a behavior that can be harder to detect.

3. **Defensiveness:** Quickness to blame others or a disproportionate level of defensiveness when questioned can signal underlying issues that may complicate treatment.

READING FAMILY DYNAMICS: THE SILENT CONTRIBUTORS

1. **Ambivalence:** Sometimes family members exhibit mixed feelings about the patient's condition, which could manifest as erratic support or inconsistent participation in treatment programs.

2. **Subtle Sabotage:** In some instances, family members may undermine treatment indirectly by offering potentially harmful advice or encouraging unhealthy behaviors while appearing supportive.

3. **Emotional Volatility:** Sudden mood swings or inconsistent emotional states among family members can reflect deeper, unresolved issues that could impact the patient's care.

THE ROLE OF CLINICAL JUDGMENT AND PEER FEEDBACK

Clinical judgment honed over years of practice enables you to interpret these subtle cues effectively. However, it's crucial to balance intuition with evidence-based practice. When you encounter difficult-to-handle situations, seeking peer feedback offers the advantage of a second lens, providing you a broader perspective to guide your approach.

Understanding that difficult behavior often manifests in less obvious ways allows you to anticipate challenges and strategize accordingly. This nuanced awareness is vital for formulating effective interventions, both for individual patients and complex family dynamics.

THE PSYCHOLOGY BEHIND DIFFICULT BEHAVIOR

While confrontations and non-compliance can be frustrating, understanding the psychological underpinnings of these behaviors can be illuminating and can guide more effective intervention strategies. This section delves into the role of mental health disorders, psychological defense mechanisms, and underlying fears that contribute to these challenges.

THE ROLE OF MENTAL HEALTH DISORDERS

1. **Personality Disorders:** Conditions like borderline personality disorder or antisocial personality disorder can cause patterns of instability, impulsivity, and sometimes manipulative or confrontational behavior. Recognizing these patterns can help tailor empathetic and boundary-setting treatment plans.

2. **Mood Disorders:** Patients with bipolar disorder or major depressive disorder can have varying levels of cooperativeness depending on their current mood state. An understanding of these shifts can help in forecasting potential issues in treatment compliance or interaction.

3. **Anxiety Disorders:** Some seemingly difficult behavior, such as excessive questioning or repeated calls to nursing stations, might stem from underlying anxiety disorders. Distinguishing this can guide the nursing staff toward a more patient-centered, reassuring approach.

PSYCHOLOGICAL DEFENSE MECHANISMS

1. **Projection:** Patients or family members might attribute their own undesirable feelings or behaviors to others, blaming nursing staff or other patients for their own shortcomings.

2. **Denial:** This often manifests itself as an outright refusal to accept a difficult reality. Family members might be in denial about the severity of a loved one's condition, leading to tensions in treatment discussions.

3. **Passive-Aggressiveness:** Rather than openly express displeasure or disagreement, some individuals might resort to indirect expression of hostility or resistance, complicating transparent communication.

UNDERLYING FEARS AND ANXIETIES

1. **Fear of Vulnerability:** The treatment setting often requires patients and families to confront uncomfortable truths, making them feel exposed or vulnerable. This fear can manifest as defensiveness or combativeness.

2. **Fear of Loss of Control:** Especially in psychiatric settings where autonomy can be restricted, patients and families might act out as a way to regain a sense of control.

3. **Existential Anxieties:** Questions around purpose, mortality, and meaning can become forefront, especially in severe or chronic cases, fueling non-compliant or confrontational behavior as a form of existential grappling.

Understanding the psychology behind difficult behavior not only enriches your clinical toolbox but also facilitates a more empathetic approach. This nuanced view allows for a more individualized treatment plan, enhancing the overall care quality.

Managing difficult behavior in a psychiatric setting often feels like walking a tightrope. On one side, there's the weight of biological predispositions—those genetic elements that tilt the scale toward impulsivity or certain mental health disorders. On the other, the pull of environmental influences such as the residue of trauma, socio-economic conditions, cultural nuances, and the immediate stressors that color a patient's world. It's this interaction between nature and nurture that forms the backdrop against which psychiatric healthcare professionals operate.

But beyond the scientific and sociological factors lies an ethical quagmire that professionals grapple with daily: where does one draw the line between enabling bad behavior and recognizing the significant strides a patient has made in their behavioral journey? This dilemma is far from academic. It has real-world implications for the safety of the healthcare environment and the patient's mental well-being. Enabling harmful patterns by failing to set boundaries could compromise both. Yet, an absence of acknowledgment for genuine progress could snuff out the fragile flame of self-improvement, demoralizing patients who are doing their best to evolve.

Striking this balance is neither simple nor formulaic. It often requires crafting highly individualized care plans that meld past histories and current realities while staying adaptable to progress or setbacks. It also benefits from the wisdom of the crowd, so to speak—a multidisciplinary team offering different perspectives can help calibrate the equilibrium between enabling and empathy. In particularly tricky cases, ethical consultations can provide that extra layer of nuanced understanding.

Through this lens, dealing with difficult behavior transcends the simplistic notion of "good" or "bad" actions. It invites healthcare providers to approach each case with a finely tuned sense of empathy, matched with a rigorous commitment to maintaining a safe and therapeutic environment. After all, the ultimate goal isn't just to manage difficult behavior but to understand its roots and help pave the road for meaningful, lasting change.

THE ART OF DE-ESCALATION

As healthcare professionals, we often find ourselves in the eye of emotional storms that can quickly spiral out of control if not effectively managed. This is especially true in psychiatric settings, where underlying mental health conditions can add layers of complexity to interactions with patients and their families. Mastering the art of de-escalation not only helps maintain a safe and harmonious environment, but it's also a crucial skill for achieving the therapeutic goals essential for patient improvement.

VERBAL AND NON-VERBAL CUES FOR CALMING TENSE SITUATIONS

Your words and even your silence carry weight. The tone, volume, and pace of your speech can either escalate a situation or bring a sense of calm. Non-verbal cues, like maintaining appropriate eye contact and adopting a non-threatening posture, can complement your verbal strategies. These signals together create a zone of psychological safety, where individuals feel less defensive and more open to dialogue.

ACTIVE LISTENING AND VALIDATION AS DE-ESCALATION TECHNIQUES

It's not enough to just hear the words; you need to listen actively, giving your full attention to the person speaking. Active listening involves nodding, summarizing what you've heard, and avoiding interruptions. By doing so, you validate the other person's experience, a crucial first step in resolving conflicts.

STEPHEN COVEY'S PRINCIPLE: FIRST SEEK TO UNDERSTAND, THEN TO BE UNDERSTOOD

Stephen Covey's principle aligns beautifully with the ethos of psychiatric care and is particularly disarming in tense situations.[1] By first striving to understand the other person's perspective, you signal a form of respect that often defuses tension. This sets the stage for a more collaborative relationship, where both parties feel acknowledged and are thus more open to understanding each other.

PRACTICAL EXERCISES FOR DE-ESCALATION

1. **Reflective Listening**: Repeat the patient's last words or main point. This not only confirms that you're engaged but also offers a pause for the other person to reflect on what they're saying.

2. **The "I-Feel" Statement**: Convey your concerns without blaming or accusing. For example, instead of saying "You are making the environment unsafe," say, "I feel concerned about the safety of everyone here."

3. **Timeouts**: A short break in the conversation can sometimes do wonders. It allows all parties to reset emotionally and intellectually, making space for more constructive dialogue to ensue.

Understanding and implementing these de-escalation techniques is vital in maintaining the integrity of the therapeutic environment. The end goal is to harmonize the psychiatric setting, making it a space where healing is not only possible but probable. This, too, embodies the core message of this book—creating spaces for meaningful conversations and authentic human connection. Through de-escalation, we don't merely resolve conflicts; we set the groundwork for meaningful therapeutic relationships that can catalyze true change.

DRAWING ON WISDOM FROM "NEVER SPLIT THE DIFFERENCE"

The world of high-stakes negotiation may seem far removed from healthcare, but there are invaluable lessons to be learned from Chris Voss's *Never Split the Difference*.[17][18] As a former FBI hostage negotiator, Voss honed his communication skills in the most high-pressure situations imaginable—where lives were literally on the line. His methods, built over decades of experience, transcend academic theory; they've been tested in the crucible of human emotion, need, and unpredictability. A key tenet that Voss emphasizes is the power of "mirroring," or repeating the last one to three words your conversation partner says. While this may sound overly simple, its impact is profound. For example, if someone says, "I'm angry with the justice system," a suitable mirrored response would be, "I hear you; you are upset with the justice system and have every right to be."

Mirroring acts as a quick and effective way to establish rapport.

In a psychiatric healthcare setting, building rapport is often the first step in creating a safe and trusting environment for both patients and families. By reflecting back what the patient or family member has said, you subtly show that you are engaged and listening, potentially leading to more meaningful exchanges and setting the stage for effective de-escalation of tensions.

Voss's principle of "tactical empathy" is another concept that finds relevance in healthcare. This goes beyond simply understanding someone's viewpoint; it's about actively vocalizing that understanding.

Saying, "I see this is tough for you," or, "I can't begin to understand your pain, but I want to help," serves to defuse emotional volatility. The power of acknowledgment can never be underestimated. It brings a level of human connection into interactions that are often charged with various emotions, and that connection can be a game-changer in a psychiatric care setting.

In this way, Voss's strategies offer an enriching dimension to the art of dealing with difficult patients and families. They serve as practical tools that complement the therapeutic aims of psychiatric care, aiming for an environment that is not just safe, but also deeply human. These are strategies that don't just work in high-stakes hostage negotiations; they can be life-changing in everyday healthcare settings as well.

While Chris Voss initially applied the concept of the "Late Night FM DJ Voice" in high-stakes situations like hostage negotiations, the application is surprisingly universal. The essence of this voice is a calm, soothing tone that has the remarkable ability to defuse tension and invite receptivity. Voss found that by employing this tranquil intonation, even individuals in the act of holding others hostage could be coaxed into lowering their defenses and engaging in more rational dialogue. The principle is just as relevant in healthcare settings. When emotions escalate and patience wanes, using the Late Night FM DJ Voice becomes an immediate, non-threatening means to de-escalate the situation. It shifts the emotional climate, encouraging the person you're communicating with to also become more open and less defensive.

It's a tactic that resonates well with the earlier point about first seeking to understand, then be understood, as outlined by Stephen Covey.

When you approach a difficult patient or their family with a voice that suggests not just authority but also tranquility, you send an immediate, unspoken message: "I am here to listen, and I am not a threat." This can be incredibly disarming and pave the way for more effective communication and problem-solving.

In this setting, you're often balancing on a fine line between showing empathy and understanding, while not enabling bad or harmful behavior. Here, Voss's approach offers a nuanced strategy. By coupling the disarming nature of the Late Night FM DJ Voice with tactical empathy and mirroring, you provide a framework within which difficult conversations can turn into constructive ones.

These techniques do more than simply get you through an interaction; they empower you to navigate the complexities of human emotion and conflict with grace. And in a field where you often find yourself in emotionally draining situations, these are not just tactics but essential skills for long-term career sustainability. Given the wide range of experiences and backgrounds that psychiatric patients come from—many of them scarred by trauma or debilitating mental health conditions—the line between enabling and empathizing can be incredibly fine.

These strategies help to negotiate that line effectively, always striving for the optimal therapeutic outcome.

Basically, what Chris Voss offers in *Never Split the Difference* can be viewed as more than negotiation techniques; they are fundamental principles of human interaction that can significantly enhance the quality of psychiatric care.

Tactical empathy goes beyond just understanding someone's feelings and perspective; it's actively acknowledging them to generate rapport and trust. By verbalizing an understanding of someone's emotions and needs, you're establishing a connection, however tenuous, an essential first step to resolving conflicts peacefully.

A famous example of tactical empathy in action can be found in the 1972 case of Tony Kiritsis, who took Richard Hall, a mortgage broker, hostage at gunpoint in Indianapolis. During the nearly 63-hour standoff, lead negotiator Lieutenant James "Bo" Dietl employed a technique akin to tactical empathy. Instead of dismissing Kiritsis as a criminal or a madman, Dietl made a conscious effort to understand and vocalize the frustration and desperation Kiritsis felt. This helped create a rapport and kept the situation from escalating further.

Dietl listened attentively to Kiritsis' grievances about the mortgage system he believed had wronged him and acknowledged his feelings of desperation and injustice. By providing Kiritsis a respectful space to voice his feelings and demonstrating understanding, Dietl managed to build enough trust to negotiate a peaceful surrender, thus avoiding a possible fatal ending for the hostage or the police.

The lessons from this real-world scenario can be translated to healthcare settings, especially in psychiatric nursing where emotions run high, and the stakes are often elevated. Understanding the emotional state of a patient or family member can create a path to meaningful dialogue, ultimately leading to a more manageable interaction. Tactical empathy becomes an essential tool in your arsenal to de-escalate difficult situations, aligning with the overarching goal of our book: becoming adept at managing complex interpersonal dynamics in healthcare settings.

As we conclude our exploration of effective communication strategies, we've uncovered the power of a calming tone, the importance of tactical empathy, and the real-world examples that highlight their effectiveness in diffusing high-stress situations. These skills are not only vital in moments of crisis but also indispensable in healthcare. In our next chapter, we go even deeper into the complex patient relationships and the delicate balance of setting boundaries. We'll explore the nuances of the fine line between connection and protection, providing you with invaluable insights to enhance your practice as a healthcare professional.

Action Step: Tactical Empathy

Begin incorporating the principles of tactical empathy into your daily interactions. Take a moment to actively listen, acknowledge the emotions of patients and families, and verbalize your understanding. This simple yet powerful act can foster trust and rapport, setting the stage for more effective communication and conflict resolution in your healthcare practice.

CHAPTER EIGHT
NAVIGATING COMPLEX PATIENT RELATIONSHIPS AND SETTING BOUNDARIES

THE DELICATE BALANCE OF CONNECTION AND PROTECTION

THE DANCE between patient relationships and professional boundaries requires grace, intuition, and continual self-awareness. How to approach this is especially crucial in professions that deal directly with human emotions and vulnerabilities.

As a psychiatric registered nurse, I find myself on the frontline of this dance daily. Individuals with personality disorders, by their very nature, often challenge and test boundaries. Their behaviors, driven by deeply ingrained patterns and coping mechanisms, can lead to situations where the establishment of clear, firm boundaries becomes not just beneficial but essential for the well-being of both patient and caregiver. However, it's crucial to note that boundary-testing isn't exclusive to those with clinical diagnoses. In our personal and professional lives, we all encounter individuals who, intentionally or otherwise, push the limits. Whether it's a persistent patient seeking additional attention, a colleague overstepping their role, or even a well-meaning family member intruding on personal matters, the need for boundary setting is a universal challenge.

This chapter aims to guide healthcare professionals through the delicate art of setting boundaries, drawing from the wisdom of experts like Dr. Cloud and intertwining it with firsthand experiences from the trenches of psychiatric nursing. The dance might be complicated, but with the right steps, we can move through it with poise and purpose.

THE POWER OF GENUINE INTERACTION

Empathy, often described as the ability to "walk a mile in someone else's shoes," is a foundational pillar in healthcare. Without it, the clinical processes and technical expertise, no matter how advanced, risk becoming mechanical, devoid of the human touch that is so crucial in the healing process.

Imagine a world where medical professionals approach their tasks with robotic precision, showing no emotion or understanding. Such an environment would lack the human warmth and connection that patients so desperately seek during vulnerable moments. Genuine, empathetic interactions serve as the bridge between clinical care and human touch. They ensure that patients feel seen, heard, and valued, not just as cases to be managed, but as individuals with unique stories, fears, and hopes.

A simple gesture, like taking an extra moment to listen or offering a word of comfort, can make a world of difference in a patient's experience. As healthcare professionals, the impact we can make by genuinely connecting with our patients extends beyond the immediate medical outcome. It builds trust, reduces anxiety, and fosters a therapeutic relationship that can significantly influence a patient's overall healing journey.

BALANCING HEART AND MIND

However, as enriching as these deep connections can be, they also present a challenge. The very nature of empathy means that caregivers open themselves up to the emotions of our patients. We feel their pain, joy, despair, and hope. While this emotional investment is what makes care truly patient-centered, it also poses the risk of blurring the lines between professional and personal involvement.

Professional detachment doesn't mean building an impenetrable wall around oneself. Instead, it signifies understanding where to draw the line. It's about recognizing that while we can deeply care about our patients and their outcomes, we must also prioritize our mental and emotional well-being. The weight of carrying every patient's emotional baggage can lead to rapid burnout, making it essential to strike a balance.

One practical approach is to practice reflective listening. This technique allows healthcare professionals to listen actively and empathetically without internalizing the emotions being expressed. It's a way of being fully present with the patient without letting their emotions consume our own.

Another strategy involves setting clear emotional boundaries. This doesn't mean becoming cold or distant but rather understanding that there's a limit to the emotional load one can carry. Regular self-check-ins, mindfulness practices, and even seeking peer or professional support can aid in maintaining this delicate balance.

In essence, the art of empathetic connection is a delicate balance between heart and mind. Many often misconceive boundaries as being cold or adopting a black-and-white stance. However, the true essence of setting boundaries lies in the ability to firmly establish them where needed, without sacrificing the warmth of empathy. It involves being deeply present with our patients, offering genuine understanding and care, while also ensuring our emotional and professional integrity. It's not distancing ourselves, but rather interacting with compassion and wisdom, ensuring our well-being and that of our patients.

RECOGNIZING THE EMOTIONAL LABOR

With healthcare, the emotional labor that comes with caring for patients day in and day out, while intangible, is very real and has profound implications on a professional's mental well-being.

Emotional labor encompasses the feelings and emotions healthcare professionals manage while on the job. It's the effort of putting on a brave face for a patient even when overwhelmed, offering reassurance when internally filled with doubt, or bearing the brunt of a patient's frustration or anguish. You must be the steady hand and the comforting voice, regardless of one's internal conflicts.

I recall a particular instance during one of my shifts. A young woman, in her early twenties, was admitted with severe depression. As I spoke with her, it became evident that she felt a profound sense of isolation and hopelessness. Her stories resonated with me, reminding me of a close friend who had undergone similar struggles. Each session with her was emotionally taxing. I had to regulate my personal feelings, ensuring they didn't overshadow the therapeutic process. After our sessions, I often found a quiet corner to reflect and regather myself, acutely aware of the emotional toll the interactions took on me.

Another time, I encountered a patient with borderline personality disorder. These individuals often have tumultuous relationship patterns and can exhibit intense episodes of anger, depression, and anxiety. During our interactions, he would swing between praising me profusely to expressing intense disdain. Handling these interactions required immense emotional control, ensuring that I did not react impulsively to his provocations.

Such instances underscore the immense emotional labor intrinsic to the healthcare profession. It's not just about administering treatments or conducting therapy sessions. It's about the silent, unseen efforts that go into managing one's emotions while providing care. The smiles that mask concern, the calm voice that hides internal turmoil, and the steady demeanor that belies exhaustion.

Recognizing this emotional labor is the first step toward addressing it. It's essential to acknowledge the emotional toll, give oneself permission to feel, and seek avenues for support and rejuvenation. Because, while emotional labor is an inherent part of healthcare, it doesn't mean professionals should bear its brunt silently and alone.

DRAWING THE LINE: THE SCIENCE AND ART OF BOUNDARY SETTING

Boundaries, in their simplest form, represent an invisible line of demarcation that separates us from others. They define what's me and what's not me. Dr. Henry Cloud, in his groundbreaking book *Boundaries*, delves into the profound significance of understanding and establishing personal boundaries.[18] He highlights how they act as a protective barrier, ensuring our emotional, mental, and physical well-being.

Concerning healthcare, boundaries take on an even more critical role. Every day, professionals are immersed in a sea of emotions, from the deep anguish of a patient receiving a terminal diagnosis to the jubilant relief of a family welcoming a newborn. These emotional waves, if unchecked, can easily sweep professionals off their feet, leading to emotional exhaustion and, ultimately, burnout.

Consider the various roles a healthcare professional plays: a listener, a guide, a comforter, a decision-maker. Each role demands emotional investment, and without clear boundaries, it becomes all too easy to lose oneself in them. A doctor might carry the sadness of a patient's diagnosis home, a nurse might constantly mull over a patient's offhand comment, and a therapist might find themselves excessively worrying about a patient's well-being outside of sessions. While these reflect a deep level of care and commitment, they also signify blurred boundaries.

In the healthcare setting, the significance of boundaries extends beyond just emotional interactions. There's the need to set boundaries with time, ensuring one doesn't consistently work beyond their scheduled hours. There's the need to set boundaries with tasks, understanding when to delegate or when to say no. And, crucially, there's the need to set boundaries with oneself, recognizing when it's time to take a break, seek support, or even take a day off.

But setting boundaries isn't about erecting impenetrable walls or becoming emotionally detached. Quite the contrary. As Dr. Cloud emphasizes, boundaries gain a sense of agency, taking responsibility for one's well-being. They allow healthcare professionals to engage empathetically, without getting enmeshed. They enable one to care deeply, without depleting themselves entirely.

Boundaries represent a delicate interplay between professional dedication and personal well-being. They are both an empirical understanding rooted in one's limits and a dynamic art, requiring ongoing adaptation based on individual circumstances. Yet, even with the most well-defined boundaries, healthcare professionals can find themselves in complex emotional territories. One such territory includes transference and countertransference, phenomena that can deeply impact patient-provider relationships and challenge even the most seasoned professionals. Understanding these interactions is crucial in maintaining the integrity of therapeutic relationships and ensuring that personal emotions do not cloud clinical judgment.

ADDRESSING TRANSFERENCE AND COUNTERTRANSFERENCE

Transference and countertransference are terms that originated from psychoanalytic therapy but have applicability across various healthcare disciplines. At its core, transference refers to the unconscious redirection of a patient's feelings about a significant person in their life onto the healthcare provider. For instance, a patient might view a doctor as a parental figure, transferring feelings of trust or distrust based on their past relationships.

Countertransference, on the other hand, is the reverse. It involves the healthcare professional projecting their own feelings onto the patient, often as a reaction to the patient's transference. It could manifest as a therapist feeling protective of a patient who reminds them of a younger sibling or a nurse feeling irritated by a patient who mirrors a challenging personal relationship.

During my time as a psychiatric registered nurse, I've encountered numerous instances of these phenomena. One particularly poignant memory is of a young patient who, due to a troubled relationship with her father, alternated between seeking approval and acting rebelliously. On numerous occasions, she expressed that I reminded her of her father. This transference sometimes made therapeutic interactions challenging, as her reactions were deeply rooted in her past experiences.

In another situation, I found myself feeling unusually frustrated with a patient who consistently dismissed medical advice. Upon reflection, I realized he reminded me of a close friend who had similarly disregarded health recommendations, leading to severe consequences.

Recognizing this countertransference was crucial, as it allowed me to separate my personal feelings from his care.

Dealing with these emotional undercurrents requires a keen sense of self-awareness and reflection. Here are some strategies that can be beneficial:

1. **Regular Supervision and Peer Review:** Discussing challenging cases with peers or supervisors can provide fresh perspectives and help in recognizing patterns of transference or countertransference.

2. **Personal Therapy:** For professionals in therapeutic roles, undergoing personal therapy can offer insights into their own emotional triggers and patterns.

3. **Continuous Education:** Engaging in workshops and courses on transference and countertransference can enhance understanding and offer tools to manage these situations.

4. **Mindfulness and Reflection:** Taking moments to introspect and assess one's feelings toward patients can help in recognizing and addressing potential biases.

Within the patient-provider relationship, understanding transference and countertransference is vital, but it's just one part of the equation. To truly navigate these complexities, a deeper introspection is required. This introspection, or self-awareness, acts as the bedrock upon which successful, therapeutic interactions are built. Recognizing our triggers and vulnerabilities isn't just beneficial—it's essential. As we explore the pivotal role of self-awareness in healthcare further, we'll emphasize the profound impact of self-reflection on maintaining harmonious patient relationships.

THE ROLE OF SELF-AWARENESS

Self-awareness is often likened to a mirror, reflecting not just our outward actions but our inner motivations, biases, and emotional responses. In the realm of healthcare, this mirror becomes especially critical. Every day, professionals encounter a plethora of emotions. Amidst the highs and lows, understanding one's emotional landscape can be the difference between effective care and unintended harm.

1. **Recognizing One's Triggers:** Everyone has certain scenarios or behaviors that elicit strong emotional responses. For a healthcare provider, it could be a patient's non-compliance, a family's anger, or even feelings of helplessness in complex cases. Recognizing these triggers allows professionals to prepare and react in a measured manner. For instance, during my tenure as a psychiatric registered nurse, I found that patients exhibiting manipulative behaviors were particularly challenging for me. Recognizing this trigger allowed me to approach such situations with added caution and seek guidance when needed.

2. **Acknowledging Vulnerabilities:** No one is immune to emotions, and vulnerabilities are a natural part of the human experience. Perhaps past experiences or personal traumas make certain patient stories resonate more deeply. By acknowledging these vulnerabilities, healthcare professionals can ensure they're not clouding their judgment.

3. **Regular Self-Reflection:** Setting aside time for introspection can be illuminating. Whether it's through journaling, meditation, or even quiet contemplation, these moments of reflection allow professionals to assess and understand their emotional responses, ensuring they remain aligned with the best interests of the patient.

4. **Seeking Feedback:** Sometimes, our self-perceptions might not align with how others perceive us. Actively seeking feedback from peers, supervisors, or even patients can provide valuable insights into areas of improvement.

5. **Professional Development and Training:** Workshops focusing on emotional intelligence and self-awareness can offer tools and tech-

niques to enhance introspection. Continuous learning in this area can significantly benefit patient-provider interactions.

Healthcare decisions can have profound implications, so the role of self-awareness cannot be overstated. By understanding and managing our emotions, biases, and triggers, healthcare professionals can ensure that their interactions remain therapeutic, compassionate, and centered on the well-being of the patient.

STRATEGIES FOR EFFECTIVE BOUNDARY SETTING

Setting boundaries, especially in the healthcare sector, is more than just saying "yes" or "no" to demands. It's about creating an environment where both the healthcare professional and the patient feel respected, understood, and valued. Dr. Henry Cloud's work on boundaries provides invaluable insights, and here, we'll explore some practical strategies inspired by his teachings, tailored for healthcare professionals.

1. **Define Your Boundaries Clearly:** Before you can enforce boundaries, you need to know what they are. Reflect on what you're comfortable with in different situations and be specific. For instance, decide on how you'll handle personal questions from patients or how much time you can allocate to each patient without compromising care.

2. **Be Consistent:** Once you've set a boundary, it's vital to be consistent in upholding it. This consistency signals to others that you're serious about your limits, and over time, it will reduce the number of boundary challenges you face.

3. **Use Clear and Assertive Communication:** When expressing your boundaries, be clear and assertive, but not aggressive. For instance, instead of saying, "I can't deal with this right now," you could say, "I need to attend to another patient now, but I'll be back to check on you shortly."

4. **Practice Saying No:** One of the most challenging aspects of boundary setting is learning to say "no" without feeling guilty. Remember, saying no is about preserving your ability to provide the best care, not about rejecting the person making the request.

5. **Seek Feedback:** Occasionally, check in with colleagues or supervisors to get feedback on your boundary-setting. They might offer insights or perspectives you hadn't considered.

ROLE-PLAYING SCENARIOS FOR BOUNDARY SETTING IN ACTION

Scenario 1: A patient has obtained your personal number and is messaging you during off-duty hours, seeking advice. *Response:* "I understand your concerns, but it's essential to contact the hospital's helpline for immediate assistance during off-duty hours. It ensures you get the right help promptly."

Scenario 2: A colleague constantly asks you to swap shifts with little notice. *Response:* "I'm willing to switch shifts occasionally with advance notice, but last-minute changes can be challenging for me. Let's plan better so it works for both of us."

Scenario 3: A patient becomes quite aggressive, demanding immediate attention and treatment, even though others need care just as urgently. *Response:* "I understand your frustration and pain, and I genuinely want to help you. Everyone here is working hard to provide care as quickly as possible. I ask for your patience, and I promise we'll attend to you as soon as we can."

Scenario 4: A patient asks to add you on a personal social media account. *Response:* "I appreciate the gesture, but I keep my professional and personal life separate. You can always reach out to the hospital's official channels if you need assistance."

As healthcare professionals strive to establish clear boundaries, they not only ensure their well-being but also enhance the quality of care they provide. Yet, even in environments where boundaries are well-respected, some challenges test the emotional resilience of every individual in the healthcare field. One of the most profound of these challenges is handling grief and loss, a topic we talk about in the following chapter.

Action Step: Boundary Review

Schedule a 15-minute self-reflection session at the end of each work week to assess your boundary-setting practices. Use this time to identify instances where you felt your boundaries were tested, either by patients or colleagues, and think of ways to communicate your boundaries more clearly in the future. This small but consistent practice will help you maintain both your professional integrity and emotional well-being.

CHAPTER NINE
NAVIGATING GRIEF AND LOSS

IN THE ECHOING hallways of hospitals and clinics, grief is an inevitable emotion that visitors experience, and where professionals witness life and death daily. While the triumphs of saved lives and successful treatments are celebrated, the moments of loss, often occurring in quiet rooms and hushed corridors, carry a weight that's felt long after the day is over.

For many healthcare professionals, these experiences become a silent collection of memories, tucked away but never truly forgotten. The passing of a long-term patient, the unexpected outcome of a surgery, or the heart-wrenching conversation with a grieving family adds a layer to the emotional tapestry of their profession. And while medical training prepares them for clinical challenges, the emotional journey of dealing with grief is a path that's often taken in solitude.

Yet, it's essential to remember that grief, while universal, manifests uniquely for everyone. For a pediatric nurse, it might be the memory of a young patient's laughter echoing in their ears. For a surgeon, it could be the reflection on what could've been done differently. And for a psychiatric nurse, it might be the emotional aftermath of a patient's traumatic story. Each experience, though distinct, underscores the profound emotional depth of the healthcare field.

As we head further into this chapter, we aim to shed light onto these tough experiences, offering both understanding and strategies to cope with grief and loss. Because in understanding our grief, we not only heal ourselves but also deepen the empathy and care we extend to our patients.

THE MULTIFACETED NATURE OF GRIEF

Grief, while universally experienced, is far from a one-size-fits-all emotion. Its manifestations are as varied as the individuals who experience it. For healthcare professionals, the unique environment they operate in exposes them to a spectrum of grief, often amplifying its impact due to the recurrent nature of loss in their field.

1. Anticipatory Grief: Before loss even occurs, grief can already start to creep in. Anticipatory grief is the deep emotion felt in expectation of loss. In healthcare, this might manifest when treating patients with terminal illnesses. The knowledge that a patient is nearing the end of their life can lead to a cascade of feelings – sorrow for the impending loss, anxiety about the impending emotional pain, and even guilt for feeling the grief before the loss has occurred. It's a preemptive mourning, where healthcare professionals may grieve for the future absence of their patient and the unfulfilled plans and potential.

2. Complicated Grief: While most people gradually find ways to come to terms with loss, some find themselves trapped in the intense emotions of grief. This prolonged form of grief, termed complicated grief, can feel just as raw and painful as when the loss first occurred. For healthcare professionals, especially those in high-stress specialties, the accumulation of multiple losses in quick succession can make the grieving process challenging. They might experience intrusive thoughts, intense sorrow, and difficulty accepting the loss, even months or years after the event.

3. Disenfranchised Grief: Not all grief is openly acknowledged or socially validated. Disenfranchised grief refers to a loss that isn't typically recognized or understood by others. In the medical field, professionals might experience this when they grieve for a patient they weren't particularly close to or for situations where the loss isn't death – for instance, witnessing a patient's decline in cognitive abilities. Because this grief isn't always validated, it can lead to feelings of isolation, where professionals might question the validity of their own emotions.

REPETITIVE LOSS IN HEALTHCARE SETTINGS

Unique to the healthcare profession is the recurring exposure to loss. Whether it's a seasoned physician or a nurse just starting out, the inevitability of patient loss is a constant. Over time, these repeated experiences can accumulate, leading to what's known as "cumulative grief." Each new loss might resurrect emotions from previous ones, making the grieving process more complex and layered. For some, it might feel like an emotional "whiplash," with little time to process one loss before facing another.

Coping with grief requires a deep understanding of its many facets. Recognizing the type of grief one is experiencing can be the first step toward processing it. In the subsequent sections, we'll dive into strategies and coping mechanisms to help healthcare professionals journey through their unique experiences of grief.

PERSONAL STORIES: MOMENTS OF HEARTBREAK AND HEALING

In the medical profession, every thread tells a story, a narrative of loss, resilience, and recovery. While the clinical aspect of medicine is often discussed, it's these personal stories that provide a window into the emotional turmoil of healthcare professionals.

DR. PAUL KALANITHI: A SURGEON'S REFLECTION ON MORTALITY AND MEANING

There are stories that transcend the confines of their context, resonating deeply with anyone who encounters them. Dr. Paul Kalanithi's journey is one of those. As a rising star in neurosurgery, Dr. Kalanithi was accustomed to life and death situations. Yet, when confronted with his own terminal lung cancer diagnosis, he was thrust into an introspective exploration of what it truly means to live. His memoir, *When Breath Becomes Air,* is a beautiful testament to this exploration, capturing the raw emotions of grappling with an imminent end while still in life's prime.[19]

For healthcare professionals, Dr. Kalanithi's narrative hits particularly close to home. Here was a colleague, a peer, suddenly on the other side of the diagnosis. The role reversal, from the doctor giving the prognosis to the patient receiving it, is a stark reminder of life's unpredictability. Every healthcare worker knows the uncertainty that looms with each patient, but seeing one of their own confront it brought a whole new depth of understanding.

But what stood out even more was Dr. Kalanithi's resilience and determination. In the face of adversity, he didn't retreat into despair.

Instead, he turned to introspection, writing, and reflection. He delved deep into the existential questions of life, purpose, and legacy. By sharing his journey, he not only offered solace and understanding to countless readers but also left an indelible mark on the medical community, reminding them of the profound human experiences behind every diagnosis.

THE RIPPLE EFFECT OF SHARED LOSS

In the tight-knit healthcare community, the loss of a patient or colleague reverberates deeply. The shared experience of grief often draws professionals closer, forging bonds in the crucible of shared heartbreak. When one nurse or doctor loses a patient, especially someone they've treated for an extended period, the entire unit feels that loss. It's a collective heartbreak, a shared sorrow that underscores the deep emotional connections healthcare professionals often form with their patients.

Yet, in this shared grief also lies shared healing. Colleagues become pillars of support, understanding the unique pain that such losses entail. They share stories, reminisce about moments of joy and laughter, and help each other through the emotional aftermath. It's a testament to the medical community's resilience and camaraderie, demonstrating that even in moments of profound sorrow, there's an opportunity for healing and growth.

COPING MECHANISMS FOR HEALTHCARE PROFESSIONALS: EMBRACING SELF-CARE DURING TIMES OF GRIEF

Grief is an emotion that knows no boundaries, rank, or specialty.

Whether seasoned or just starting out, loss is felt universally in the healthcare profession. Yet, amidst the rapid pace and demanding nature of their roles, healthcare professionals often find little room to process these emotions, let alone heal from them. This is where the importance of proactive self-care comes into play.

Self-care, especially during times of grief, is a necessity. It's about recognizing and honoring one's own emotional and mental well-being amidst the relentless tide of patient care. This could manifest in various ways:

1. **Scheduled Breaks**: Even brief moments of respite, such as a short walk outside the hospital or a few minutes of quiet reflection in a lounge, can make a difference. It's a chance to breathe, recalibrate, and momentarily distance oneself from the immediate environment.

2. **Mindfulness and Meditation**: Techniques like deep breathing, progressive muscle relaxation, or guided imagery can anchor the mind and offer solace. Incorporating mindfulness practices, even if just for a few minutes daily, can help in staying centered.

3. **Journaling**: Writing can be therapeutic. Documenting feelings, experiences, or even just the day's events can provide an outlet for pent-up emotions. Over time, these entries can also serve as a testament to one's resilience and growth.

4. **Engaging in Hobbies**: Whether it's reading, painting, playing a musical instrument, or any other passion, immersing oneself in a hobby can serve as a welcome distraction. It not only provides a break from the routine but also helps in reconnecting with oneself.

5. **Physical Activity**: The benefits of exercise extend beyond physical health. A brisk walk, a kickboxing class, or even a short workout can

release endorphins, the body's natural mood lifters.

Grief, by its very nature, is a deeply personal experience. What brings comfort to one person might not resonate with another. Thus, it's crucial for each individual to find what resonates with them best.

However, the emphasis should always be on allowing oneself the grace and space to grieve, while also seeking avenues to heal and rejuvenate.

The role of healthcare professionals is undeniably challenging, but in the pursuit of caring for others, it's imperative not to overlook one's own well-being. By embracing self-care, especially during times of grief, they not only bolster their own resilience but also enhance their capacity to provide compassionate care to others.

The aftermath of particularly challenging cases can leave a lasting emotional imprint on those involved. Whether it's an unexpected outcome, a critical incident, or a particularly distressing patient story, these moments can weigh heavily on the minds of healthcare professionals. This is where the role of debriefing sessions becomes invaluable.

Debriefing sessions, often facilitated by experienced peers or counselors, offer a structured environment where healthcare professionals can discuss, reflect upon, and process their feelings about specific cases. These sessions serve multiple purposes:

1. **Validation of Emotions**: One of the most immediate benefits of debriefing is the validation it offers. Being in a space where one's feelings, whether of sadness, frustration, or even guilt, are acknowledged can be profoundly comforting.

2. **Collective Processing**: Sharing experiences with colleagues involved in the same case or scenario can lead to a collective understanding. There's a shared sense of camaraderie, knowing that others too have felt similar emotions or faced similar challenges.

3. **Learning Opportunities**: Beyond emotional processing, debriefing sessions can also be a platform for learning. By discussing what went

well and what could have been done differently, professionals can glean insights that can be applied in future scenarios.

4. **Emotional Release**: Simply talking about a challenging event can, in itself, be cathartic. Verbalizing feelings and experiences can serve as an emotional release, preventing the buildup of pent-up emotions.

5. **Preventing Burnout**: Regular debriefing can be a proactive measure against burnout. By addressing emotional challenges head-on and in a timely manner, healthcare professionals can prevent these feelings from accumulating and leading to larger issues down the line.

6. **Building Resilience**: Over time, consistent reflection and processing through debriefing sessions can bolster resilience. Professionals become better equipped to handle challenging situations, knowing they have the tools and support to process them afterward.

THE ROLE OF COMMUNITY AND PEER SUPPORT: HARNESSING THE STRENGTH OF COLLECTIVE EMPATHY

Challenging cases, long hours, and high stakes weave together, revealing an underlying strength that often goes uncelebrated: the power of community and peer support. For healthcare professionals, the journey is not one undertaken in isolation but as part of a larger, interconnected community. It's within this community that many find solace, understanding, and an unmatched depth of support.

There's an innate comfort in knowing that someone else truly understands what you're going through. Fellow healthcare professionals, whether nurses, doctors, technicians, or therapists, have walked similar paths. They've faced intense responsibility, the sorrow of loss, and the joy of a patient's recovery. This shared experience creates a bond that's profound and supportive.

Group therapy sessions, specifically designed for healthcare professionals, offer a structured environment to explore feelings, challenges, and triumphs. Led by skilled facilitators, these sessions allow participants to delve deep into their experiences, drawing strength from collective sharing and learning. It's a space where vulnerabilities are not just accepted but embraced, leading to holistic healing.

Moreover, the best counsel sometimes comes from someone who's been in your shoes. Peer counseling initiatives within healthcare institutions provide an avenue for professionals to seek guidance, advice, or simply a listening ear from colleagues. This peer-led approach often breaks down barriers, allowing for candid, heart-to-heart conversations. Beyond formal settings, there are numerous support networks and communities, both online and offline, dedicated to healthcare professionals. These spaces, from forums to dedicated helplines, offer a sense of belonging and serve as a reminder that no matter how isolating a particular challenge might feel, there's a community out there ready to lend support.

In healthcare, it's easy to get lost in the magnitude of responsibilities and overlook the small victories. But community and peer support play a pivotal role in celebrating these moments. This could be a patient's smile, a successful procedure, or simply making it through a tough day. They boost morale and foster a positive work environment.

BUILDING RESILIENCE IN THE FACE OF LOSS: CULTIVATING EMOTIONAL STRENGTH THROUGH SELF-AWARENESS AND REFLECTION

Inside a hospital or clinic, the pendulum of emotions swings back and forth. Healthcare professionals often stand as silent witnesses to the human condition's fragility, and they too are touched deeply by the spectrum of experiences they encounter. In such an emotionally charged environment, resilience, as we have discussed in depth in previous chapters, becomes an even more essential armor.

Resilience is often misunderstood as an innate quality that one either possesses or lacks. In reality, it's a skill cultivated over time and honed through experiences. It's about developing the capacity to bounce back from setbacks, find meaning in adversity, and continue moving forward with hope and determination.

One of the foundational cornerstones of resilience is self-awareness. By understanding our emotional triggers, recognizing our patterns of thought and behavior, and discerning our vulnerabilities, we equip ourselves to navigate challenging situations more adeptly. For instance, a healthcare professional who is acutely aware of their emotional response to pediatric cases, given personal experiences or inclinations, can take proactive measures to ensure they are mentally and emotionally prepared when such cases arise. Reflection plays a pivotal role in enhancing self-awareness. After a particularly harrowing day or a case that hits too close to home, setting aside time for introspection can be therapeutic. This could be in the form of journaling, meditative practices, or even simple contemplation. Such reflective practices allow professionals to process their emotions, understand their reactions, and gain clarity. It's not about changing the past but about equipping oneself better for the future.

Another technique to bolster resilience is the practice of grounding. Whenever overwhelmed by emotion, grounding exercises, such as focused breathing, tactile engagement, or reciting a calming mantra, can help anchor the mind and prevent it from spiraling. These techniques, while simple, can be profoundly effective in the heat of the moment. Furthermore, embracing a growth mindset where challenges are viewed as opportunities for growth rather than insurmountable obstacles can be transformative. When faced with loss or adversity, asking oneself, "What can I learn from this?" or "How can I grow as a result of this experience?" shifts the perspective from despair to one of empowerment.

Yet, even as healthcare professionals develop resilience, it's crucial to remember that it's okay to seek support. Resilience doesn't equate to facing challenges alone but knowing when to lean on others, when to share, and when to take a step back for self-care. In the end, the journey through healthcare, with its peaks of joy and valleys of sorrow, is a testament to the human spirit's indomitable strength. By fostering resilience, professionals not only safeguard their mental well-being but also ensure they remain the pillars of strength their patients so dearly rely on. The healthcare professional's journey is marked by moments of intense emotion, challenges, and triumphs. While grief and loss are inescapable, it also offers an opportunity for growth, introspection, and resilience. It's crucial to remember that our professional evolution isn't limited to emotional realms alone. Just as we continuously hone our emotional and interpersonal skills, our intellectual and clinical skills demand equal attention. This seamless integration of emotional resilience with ongoing learning sets the stage for the next chapter: the indispensable role of continuing education and growth in a healthcare professional's life.

Action Step

Take a moment to introspect and identify your core passion that drew you to the healthcare field. Whether it was a personal experience, an inspiring individual, or a profound desire to make a difference, reconnect with that foundational drive. This week, set aside 30 minutes to read or listen to a segment from Ray Dalio's "Principles." As you engage with his insights, reflect on how they resonate with your personal and professional journey. Consider integrating one principle into your daily routine, whether it's practicing radical transparency in your communications or valuing the input of colleagues in decision-making processes. By actively reconnecting with your passion and applying transformative principles, you can set the stage for continuous personal and professional growth.

CHAPTER TEN
THE ROLE OF CONTINUING EDUCATION AND GROWTH

THE ROLE of Passion in Mental Well-being

Amidst the daily hustle and bustle, the endless charts, the demanding patients, and the administrative tasks, it's easy for healthcare professionals to lose sight of the passion that initially drew them to the field. The intrinsic motivation and genuine desire to make a difference can sometimes get buried under layers of bureaucracy, fatigue, and work-related stress. However, reconnecting with this passion is paramount, not just for job satisfaction but also for one's mental well-being.

Remember the time when the idea of joining the healthcare field first ignited a spark within you? Maybe it was a personal experience, an inspiring individual, or simply a deep-rooted desire to help and heal. That initial drive is the antidote to burnout. It serves as a reminder of why you chose this profession and provides a sense of purpose that goes beyond the paycheck.

But how does one go about reigniting this passion, especially during challenging times?

The key lies in self-reflection and intentional action. Setting aside dedicated time to introspect and burrow deep into one's motivations and aspirations can provide clarity. Journaling, meditation, or even simple contemplative walks can aid in this process. Think about the moments in your career that filled you with pride and satisfaction. What were the common threads in those instances? Identifying these can provide insights into what truly drives you.

Furthermore, seeking out opportunities that align with these motivations can be immensely fulfilling. Perhaps it's mentoring new entrants in the field, engaging in community outreach, or even spearheading a new initiative at your workplace. Actively pursuing projects that resonate with your core beliefs and passions can rekindle the enthusiasm that might have waned over time.

However, it's essential to remember that passion is not a constant; it ebbs and flows. And that's okay. What's crucial is to acknowledge these fluctuations and take proactive measures to realign with one's purpose.

THE TANGIBLE BENEFITS OF ALIGNING PASSION WITH PROFESSION

The marriage of passion and profession is often romanticized, but its benefits extend beyond mere job satisfaction. Aligning one's intrinsic motivation with their daily tasks can have profound effects on both mental health and overall performance in the workplace.

1. Enhanced Resilience: When we are deeply passionate about our work, we are better equipped to handle challenges and setbacks. This intrinsic motivation acts as a buffer against burnout and helps us navigate stressful situations with a sense of purpose. When we believe in the value of our work and its impact on society, we're more likely to persevere through difficult times.

2. Improved Work Performance: Passion drives excellence. When we genuinely love what we do, we're more inclined to go the extra mile, innovate, and continuously improve. This not only results in personal growth but also elevates the quality of care provided to patients.

3. Greater Job Satisfaction: Naturally, when passion and profession align, job satisfaction increases. This sense of fulfillment can positively impact mental well-being, reducing feelings of monotony and the looming dread of the 'Sunday night blues.'

4. Enhanced Work-Life Balance: When we derive joy from our work, it no longer feels like a mere obligation. This can lead to a healthier work-life balance, where one doesn't feel the need to 'escape' from work but rather sees it as an integral, enjoyable part of one's life.

5. A Stronger Sense of Community: Passion is contagious. When one individual is genuinely passionate about their role, it can inspire and uplift those around them. This can foster a sense of camaraderie, mutual respect, and a collaborative work environment.

However, it's essential to strike a balance. While passion is a potent force, it's crucial to ensure it doesn't lead to overextension or personal neglect. Setting boundaries, practicing self-care, and regularly checking in with oneself can help maintain this equilibrium.

PRACTICAL STEPS TO REALIGN WITH ONE'S PASSION

Ray Dalio's "Principles" offers a treasure trove of insights into achieving success in both personal and professional spheres.[20] One of the central tenets Dalio emphasizes is the intertwining of meaningful work with meaningful relationships. In the context of healthcare professionals, this principle becomes particularly poignant.

Meaningful Work: For many in the healthcare field, their work involving healing, caring, and making tangible differences in the lives of patients is inherently meaningful. However, the day-to-day challenges can sometimes cloud this bigger picture. Dalio's emphasis on viewing one's work as a mission resonates deeply here. By continuously aligning with the fundamental purpose of aiding and healing, healthcare professionals can navigate the daily hurdles with a clearer perspective and renewed vigor.

Moreover, Dalio speaks about setting clear goals and embracing failures as learning opportunities. In a setting where mistakes can have significant consequences, this principle can be applied by fostering a culture of continuous learning, feedback, and improvement. By viewing setbacks not as failures but as steppingstones, healthcare professionals can evolve in their roles and provide even better care.

Meaningful Relationships: Dalio underscores the importance of transparent communication and building trust in fostering meaningful relationships. In the pressure-cooker medical environment, these principles become paramount. Open communication cannot only improve team dynamics but also lead to better patient outcomes.

Furthermore, Dalio's idea of "believability-weighted decision making" can be a game-changer in healthcare settings. By valuing the input of each team member, based on their expertise and experience, decisions can be more holistic and effective.

But beyond the professional setting, Dalio's emphasis on meaningful relationships serves as a reminder for healthcare professionals to cultivate deep, genuine connections outside of work. As previously discussed, these bonds, separate from the pressures of the job, can serve as a sanctuary, a source of rejuvenation, and a buffer against burnout.

Bridging the Two: Dalio's principles aren't just theoretical; they offer actionable insights. By actively seeking out meaningful work projects, continuously realigning with one's purpose in the healthcare field, and fostering transparent, trust-based relationships both in and out of the workplace, healthcare professionals can enhance their mental well-being and job satisfaction.

Essentially, Dalio's "Principles" serve as a roadmap, guiding healthcare professionals toward a fulfilling career, enriched by genuine relationships, and underpinned by a deep sense of purpose.

Despite the daily grind and challenges, it's essential to remember why one entered this profession in the first place.

1. Rediscovering Purpose: Every healthcare professional began their journey with a purpose. Maybe it was a personal experience, a desire to help, or simply the allure of the medical field. Reconnecting with his initial motivation can provide a renewed sense of direction and enthusiasm.

2. Daily Affirmations: Starting the day by reminding oneself of the impact of their work can set a positive tone. Whether it's a note on the mirror, a quick meditation session, or just some deep thinking, these daily affirmations can serve as a grounding anchor.

3. Celebrating Small Wins: In a field where life-altering decisions are the norm, it's easy to overlook the smaller achievements. Acknowledging and celebrating these small wins can instill consistent motivation. Maybe it's a patient's smile, a thank-you note, a problem solved, or even a successful procedure.

4. Continuous Learning: The medical field is ever evolving. By staying updated with the latest research, attending seminars, and engaging in discussions, professionals can ensure their work remains impactful and relevant.

In the dynamic realm of healthcare, where new discoveries and advancements are a constant, the essence of learning never truly ends. But beyond the clinical knowledge and technical proficiencies, there lies a deeper, more personal form of growth—a kind that fortifies the mind and spirit, especially in a field as demanding as healthcare. For healthcare professionals, the journey doesn't conclude once the diploma is awarded, or the initial training is complete.

The real voyage lies in the continual adaptation, evolution, and self-enhancement amidst the ever-changing medical topography. This not only ensures top-tier patient care but also nurtures the well-being of the caregiver. Let's explore the symbiotic relationship between personal growth and professional excellence, underscoring how continued education becomes a beacon of resilience, rejuvenation, and fulfillment for those in the healthcare profession.

THE TRANSFORMATIVE POWER OF PASSION

The story of Dr. Magdi Yacoub, a globally renowned cardiac surgeon, is a shining testament to the transformative power of passion in healthcare. Born in Egypt, Dr. Yacoub's journey into medicine was deeply personal. He lost his aunt to heart failure at a young age, a tragedy that would catalyze his lifelong dedication to fighting heart disease.

After training in London, Dr. Yacoub rapidly became one of the world's leading heart surgeons. But beyond his surgical skills, it was his insatiable passion for medicine and improving patient care that stood out. He performed the UK's first combined heart and lung transplant and was involved in pioneering surgeries that pushed the boundaries of what was medically possible. His innovations and techniques revolutionized cardiac surgery, saving countless lives.

Yet, despite his accolades in the West, Dr. Yacoub's heart remained with his homeland. He was deeply troubled by the lack of advanced medical facilities in Egypt and the broader African continent. Instead of simply lamenting the problem, his passion drove him to act. He founded the Aswan Heart Centre in Egypt, a state-of-the-art facility providing free cardiac care to those in need. Furthermore, he established training programs, ensuring that his knowledge and expertise would be passed on to the next generation of African doctors.

For Dr. Yacoub, medicine was never just a job—it was a calling. His unwavering commitment and passion for cardiac care have not only changed the lives of his patients but have also influenced entire generations of doctors. His story underscores the profound impact passion can have on one's career. When driven by genuine love and dedication for one's profession, challenges become surmountable, innovations arise, and the effects of one's work can be felt far and wide. Dr. Yacoub's journey is a vivid reminder that with passion, remarkable change is possible.

THE MARRIAGE OF PASSION AND PROFESSION

Dr. Magdi Yacoub's journey highlights the profound synergy that can arise when passion and profession intertwine. For many in the healthcare field, the two are inseparably linked, each fueling the other in a symbiotic embrace. This union, however, extends beyond just renowned figures in medicine; it is a sentiment that resonates with countless healthcare professionals across the globe.

1. **Enhanced Resilience:** When passion underpins our professional pursuits, we inherently develop a stronger resilience to challenges. The intrinsic motivation, much like Dr. Yacoub's devotion to cardiac care, acts as a buffer against the trials and tribulations of the profession. It provides a clarity of purpose, enabling healthcare professionals to navigate the most stressful situations with a renewed sense of mission.

2. **Elevated Performance:** Genuine passion is a catalyst for excellence. When healthcare professionals are deeply invested in their work, they are more inclined to innovate, continually learn, and strive for the best outcomes. This drive not only propels personal growth but also enhances the quality of care provided to patients.

3. **Deepened Job Satisfaction:** The alignment of passion and profession naturally leads to increased job satisfaction. When daily tasks resonate with one's core beliefs and interests, work shifts from being a mere obligation to a source of profound fulfillment.

4. **Holistic Work-Life Balance:** Passion for one's profession can redefine the work-life balance. Instead of viewing work as a draining necessity, it becomes an integral, enriching part of life. This perspective shift can lead to a more harmonious balance between personal and professional commitments. What did Mark Twain and Confucius once say? Oh yeah, "Find a job you love, and you'll never have to work a day in your life."

5. **Fostering a Vibrant Community:** Just as Dr. Yacoub's fervor inspired entire generations of doctors, an individual's passion within a healthcare facility can be infectious. It fosters a collaborative and supportive environment where team members uplift each other, driven by a shared dedication to healthcare.

As we reflect on the powerful narrative of Dr. Yacoub and countless others who embody the marriage of passion and profession, it becomes evident that this union is the heartbeat of healthcare, the force that drives innovation, instills resilience, and most importantly, ensures that the care provided is rooted in genuine empathy and dedication. As healthcare professionals, recognizing and nurturing this marriage is pivotal for both personal well-being and the broader betterment of patient care.

REDISCOVERING PURPOSE AND CELEBRATING ACHIEVEMENTS

Healthcare professionals often find themselves caught up in the web of duty and responsibility. But beneath these layers of routine and responsibility lies the original purpose that ignited their journey into healthcare. It's a flame that, while it may flicker amidst the challenges, never truly goes out.

Dr. Yacoub's story and the tales of countless others stand testament to the power of passion. However, to ensure that this passion doesn't wane, it becomes crucial to periodically reconnect with one's foundational purpose. Why did you choose this path? Was it a personal experience, an innate desire to heal, or perhaps an inspiring mentor who left an indelible mark? Rummaging through these memories can reignite the spark, illuminating the path forward even on the most challenging days.

Yet, while introspection plays a vital role in rediscovering purpose, it's equally crucial to celebrate the milestones and achievements, no matter how small. Every patient's smile, every successful diagnosis, every moment of relief witnessed are testaments to the impact of one's work. Celebrating these moments serves as a reminder of the profound difference healthcare professionals make in the lives of their patients. It's not only the grand achievements but also the small, everyday victories that cumulatively define a career filled with purpose.

In the relentless healthcare environment, these moments of reflection and celebration become the anchors of stability. They offer a respite, a moment to breathe, and most importantly, a chance to realign with the core values that define the noble profession of healthcare.

As we progress in our healthcare careers, let us remember to pause, reflect, and celebrate. For in these moments, we not only rediscover our purpose but also fortify our passion, ensuring that we continue to provide care with unwavering dedication and empathy.

BRIDGING PERSONAL GROWTH WITH PROFESSIONAL EXCELLENCE

The intersection of personal growth and professional excellence is a delicate balance that healthcare professionals engage in throughout their careers. Within this dynamic interplay lies the potential for not only professional success but also personal fulfillment.

Enter Ray Dalio's *Principles,* a beacon that illuminates the path to this harmonious blend. Dalio's insights pivot around the powerful synergy of meaningful work and authentic relationships. For healthcare professionals, this isn't merely theoretical. The essence of their work revolves around genuine human connections, and the outcomes they strive for are deeply meaningful.

The beauty of Dalio's principles lies in their universality. They encourage introspection and growth, urging individuals to continuously realign with their core values and purpose. With healthcare, this translates to a more profound connection with patients, a more collaborative relationship with peers, and a rejuvenated sense of purpose with every sunrise.

For instance, when Dalio talks about transparent communication and building trust, it reminds healthcare professionals of the importance of clear dialogues with patients and their families. Such transparency can lead to more informed decisions, better patient outcomes, and a more fulfilling professional experience.

Moreover, by valuing each team member's input, based on their expertise and experiences, decisions in healthcare settings can become more holistic, patient-centered, and effective. This collaborative environment not only elevates the quality of care but also fosters personal growth and satisfaction among healthcare workers.

In essence, by intertwining the insights from "Principles" with the unique challenges and rewards of the healthcare profession, professionals can carve a path that marries personal growth with professional excellence. This harmonious blend ensures that every day in the hospital, clinic, or field is not just about performing tasks but about evolving, learning, and making a genuine difference.

Action Step

Set aside some quiet time for yourself, preferably in a place where you feel at peace. Reflect on a moment of grief or loss you've experienced in your professional journey. Write down your feelings, the challenges you faced, and how you coped. Beside each emotion or challenge, note down a coping mechanism or support strategy discussed in this chapter that resonated with you or that you wish to explore further. Keep this written reflection as a touchstone, a personal testament to your resilience, and a guide for when you encounter moments of grief in the future.

CONCLUSION

In the demanding realm of healthcare, the journey from understanding the intricacies of the human body to navigating the complexities of the human mind can often be overwhelming. This book has aimed to shed light on the many facets of mental well-being, emphasizing the importance of self-care for those who dedicate themselves to caring for others.

From the nuances of resilience and emotional regulation to the profound insights on continuous growth and passion, each chapter underscores the significance of nurturing one's mental and emotional health. Healthcare, with its unique blend of highs and lows, demands individuals who are not only technically adept but also equipped to handle the emotional and psychological pressures that come with the territory.

The stories shared, strategies discussed, and principles explored throughout these pages are not just theoretical concepts. They serve as guiding lights, offering actionable steps for those navigating the often-tumultuous waters of the medical profession. The journey, while challenging, is also deeply rewarding, and it's essential to remember that

CONCLUSION

you're part of a broader community—a collective of healthcare professionals all striving toward a shared goal: healing and being healed.

Let this book stand as a testament to the power of self-awareness, resilience, and continuous growth. Amidst the long shifts, challenging patients, and administrative workload, there lies a deeper purpose and a calling. By prioritizing mental well-being, embracing self-care, and continually seeking growth, it's possible to find balance, purpose, and joy in the profession.

To every healthcare professional reading this, your dedication, resilience, and unwavering commitment to the well-being of others is both recognized and deeply appreciated. Here's to finding strength, rekindling passion, and making a lasting difference in the lives of countless individuals. Remember to always take a moment for yourself, for in healing oneself, you better heal others.

I hope "Self-Care Rx for Healthcare Professionals: Proven Strategies to Combat Stress and Burnout" has enriched your journey towards wellness. Your reviews not only help us reach more people but also provide invaluable feedback. I personally read each review, valuing your unique perspective in this mission.

Please take a moment to leave a review wherever you purchased this book and share how the book has impacted your approach to self-care.

Now for one final action step: I invite you to visit www.self-care-rx.com. There, you can leave a comment on one of the blog articles, providing feedback. I'd love to hear how the article relates to your specific experiences in healthcare. Your engagement and insights are a significant contribution to our community's journey towards better health and shared understanding.

Thank you for your time, your invaluable work, and your commitment to nurturing your own well-being.

ACKNOWLEDGMENTS

Navigating the complex landscape of healthcare, with its demands and challenges, is a journey seldom undertaken alone. The creation of this book was no different, and I owe a deep debt of gratitude to many who have supported, inspired, and guided me along the way.

To my wife, Libby, your unwavering support and belief in this project have been my pillars of strength. Your insights, both as a partner and a healthcare professional, enriched the narrative in ways I couldn't have imagined.

To Jackson, our bright ray of hope, you serve as a daily reminder of why it's essential to foster well-being and resilience, ensuring that we can be our best selves for the ones we love.

Oakley, our calm Australian Shepherd, you've been a source of joy and relaxation, reminding me of the simple pleasures of life amidst the chaos.

My gratitude also extends to my colleagues, mentors, and countless healthcare professionals who shared their stories, insights, and experiences. Their contributions provided depth and authenticity to the narrative, bridging the gap between theory and practice.

To the dedicated professionals at the psychiatric facility where I work, I am humbled daily by your commitment, even among a challenging bureaucratic environment. Your stories, challenges, and victories were the bedrock upon which this book was built.

Last but not least, I extend my heartfelt thanks to you, the reader. Your commitment to your profession, your quest for balance and well-being, and your dedication to making a difference inspired every word on these pages. This book is as much yours as it is mine.

With deepest appreciation, Chris.

ABOUT THE AUTHOR

Nestled in the heart of Salem, Oregon, Chris Wagner is more than an RN; he embodies the spirit of a lifelong learner. With a background in psychiatric nursing, he dedicates his experience to uplifting his community. Alongside his nursing duties, Chris has an interest in personal finance and enjoys practicing martial arts, notably Muay Thai and Brazilian Jiu-Jitsu. This blend of skills highlights Chris's balance of analytical strength and artistic passion.

Over the years, encounters with diverse individuals and intricate life stories have fueled his passion for writing, shedding light on the myriad experiences in the mental health sector. His stories shed light on the diverse experiences of his patients, highlighting the genuine challenges of psychiatric care alongside the resilience they demonstrate.

Chris, a devoted family man, often incorporates nuances of fatherhood and the spirited moments with a dynamic canine into his tales. While his writing predominantly touches upon introspective themes, glimpses of his passion for finance occasionally shine through. His work provides strategies for healthcare professionals navigating the challenges of stress and burnout.

With his wife Libby, who shares his nursing background, their young Jackson, and spirited Australian Shepherd Oakley, Chris embarks continuously on explorations of writing and inspiration. Explore further into his world on his blog: self-care-rx.com

BIBLIOGRAPHY

1. Sarıkaya, N. A., Öztürk, S., Öz, S., & Elmas, S. (2022). Emotional reactivity and burnout in clinical nurses. *Journal of Psychiatric Nursing, 13*(3).
2. Covey, S. R. (1989). *The 7 habits of highly effective people: powerful lessons in personal change.* Simon & Schuster.
3. Walker, M. (2017). *Why we sleep: Unlocking the power of sleep and dreams.* Scribner.
4. Clear, J. (2018). *Atomic habits: An easy & proven way to build good habits & break bad ones.* Avery.
5. Keller, G., & Papasan, J. (2012). *The one thing.* Bard Press.
6. David, S. (2016). *Emotional agility.* Avery.
7. Easter, M. D. (2021). *The comfort crisis.* Penguin Random House.
8. Patrick, R. P. (2022, April 1). *Cold-water immersion and cryotherapy: Neuroendocrine and fat browning effects.* FoundMyFitness. https://www.foundmyfitness.com/episodes/cold-shock-norepinephrine
9. Ketelhut, S., Querciagrossa, D., Bisang, X., Metry, X., Borter, E., & Nigg, C. (2023, October 16). *The effectiveness of the Wim Hof method on cardiac autonomic function, blood pressure, arterial compliance, and different psychological parameters.* Nature. https://www.nature.com/articles/s41598-023-44902-0&#8203
10. Chen, P. (2007). *Final exam: A surgeon's reflections on mortality.* Knopf.
11. Louv, R. (2008). *Last child in the woods: Saving our children from nature-deficit disorder.* Algonquin Books.
12. Park, B. J., Tsunetsugu, Y., Kasetani, T., Kagawa, T., & Miyazaki, Y. (2010). The physiological effects of Shinrin-yoku (taking in the forest atmosphere or forest bathing): Evidence from field experiments in 24 forests across Japan. *Environmental Health and Preventive Medicine, 15*(1), 18-26
13. Atchley, R. A., Strayer, D., & Atchley, P. (2012). Creativity in the wild: Improving creative reasoning through immersion in natural settings. *PLOS ONE, 7*(12), e51474.
14. Ramsey, D. (2010). *The total money makeover: A proven plan for financial fitness.* Thomas Nelson Publishers.
15. Puterman, E., Haritatos, J., Adler, N., Sidney, S., Schwartz, J., & Epel, E. (2013). Indirect effect of financial strain on daily cortisol output through daily negative to positive affect index in the Coronary Artery Risk Development in Young Adults Study. *Psychoneuroendocrinology, 38*(12), 2883-2889
16. Holt-Lunstad, J. (2018). The potential public health relevance of social isolation and loneliness: Prevalence, epidemiology, and risk factors. *Public Policy & Aging Report, 27*(4), 127–130.
17. Voss, C. (2016). *Never split the difference: Negotiating as if your life depended on it.* Harper Business.
18. Cloud, H., & Townsend, J. (2017). *Boundaries: When to say yes, how to say no to take control of your life.* Zondervan.

BIBLIOGRAPHY

19. Kalanithi, P. (2016). *When breath becomes air*. Random House.
20. Dalio, R. (2017). *Principles: Life and work*. Simon & Schuster

Printed in Dunstable, United Kingdom